103

198

KEVIN CALLAN'S STORY

KEVIN CALLAN'S STORY

Kevin Callan

LITTLE, BROWN AND COMPANY

A *Little, Brown* Book

First published in Great Britain in 1997
by Little, Brown and Company

Copyright © Kevin Callan 1997

The moral right of the author has been asserted.

A CIP catalogue record for this book
is available from the British Library.

ISBN 0 316 88313 1

Typeset in Janson by M Rules
Printed and bound in Great Britain
by Creative Print and Design (Wales), Ebbw Vale

UK companies, institutions and other organisations wishing
to make bulk purchases of this or any other book published
by Little, Brown should contact their local bookshop or the
special sales department at the address below.
Tel 0171 911 8000. Fax 0171 911 8100.

Little, Brown and Company (UK)
Brettenham House
Lancaster Place
London WC2E 7EN

In memory of Amanda

ACKNOWLEDGEMENTS

Les and I are very well matched as can be seen in the strength we had to show in the face of adversity. What else can I possibly say other than a massive thank you to her for her devotion. I would have loved her to have been there at the beginning but I understand that she also had a nightmare of her own to contend with.

It would take forever to thank all those directly involved in my case. I shall, therefore, mention the main people:

Campbell Malone for his great and continued support of Les and me. He had to put up with a lot as I strived for truth.

Linda Harrison for her tireless efforts on my case. How she coped with my phone calls, I'll never know.

Michael Mansfield QC for his supreme presentation of my case at the appeal. No QC could have done a better job.

Philip Wrightson, I thank you from the very bottom of my heart for your tuition, patience and lots of understanding.

To Helen Whitwell, another massive and heartfelt thank you.

The campaign groups who supported me – Innocent, Liberty, Conviction – another thank you.

To each and every person who took the trouble to follow the case, I thank you all. I am indebted to every one of you. God bless you all and may you live in peace.

FOREWORD

....

'I SEE NO reason to grant such a long extension of time. I would not have granted leave in any event. It was open to your advisers to obtain this (new) evidence at the time of your trial. The fact that two new experts have now been discovered does not enable you to reopen the matter in my opinion.'

So wrote Lord Justice Tucker on the very anniversary of Amanda's death when turning down Kevin Callan's initial application for leave to appeal (against his conviction for murder), based on evidence he had personally researched and discovered and which ultimately resulted in a successful appeal, uncontested by the Crown.

In one stroke of the pen can be seen the real and ever-present serious shortcomings of our system of criminal justice. It was confidently being predicted after the well documented, high-profile approach of the Birmingham 6, the Guildford 4, the Tottenham 3, Judith Ward, the Maguire 7, Stephen Kiszko that such miscarriages were 'a thing of the past', unlikely to return. A Royal Commission established in their wake was supposed to make proposals which would help to make such travesties a rare phenomenon. The reality is that both then and now those responsible for the administration of criminal justice have dismally failed to recognise the shortcomings inherent in the system itself.

Kevin's case, and his book, is a timely reminder of how serious the situation has become. Because it did not attract the publicity and attention it deserved there was a risk that the lessons to be learned would go unheeded. Once more, it is the victim who has managed to place on record the measure of injustice for all to see.

For me, his example is, in a way, the most telling of all. Although, fortunately, he did not spend sixteen years in prison, it is only by a whisker that such a calamity was avoided. That whisker was Kevin himself. The criminal justice system up to that point did nothing, quite the reverse.

At every stage, the problems that have beset so may other cases arose once more. Gross assumptions, misconceptions and preconceptions were displayed by the investigating police. The grand advocates, both political and legal, who recently swept away one more fundamental right – the right to silence – did so on the basis that 'innocence will always speak'. Kevin did, repeatedly asserting that he was not responsible for Amanda's death. To no avail. Such demands were merely treated as grist to the mill.

Despite having been charged with murder, his was an obvious case for bail. In the event, he remained in custody throughout the remand period between arrest in 1991 and conviction in 1992. A far from satisfactory position in which to face a trial for your life.

But the worst was yet to come. Essentially, the case against Kevin depended on the opinion of experts: that the injuries to her head, primarily a double haematoma, were caused by shaking, not by a combination of accidental falls and collisions occasioned by the cerebral palsy of the four year old and spastic diplegia. She could only speak a few words and she could only walk a few steps with the aid of splints. There was clear evidence, particularly from Amanda's mother, that Kevin loved Amanda dearly.

No one, either before the trial or during the trial, whether they be lawyer, judge, police officer, junior or medical expert, noted that the opinions sought had not been obtained from the appropriate field of medical expertise. The cannot be written of as 'nobody's fault', just as an unhappy but unforeseeable event. It represents a long-standing unwillingness to ensure proper resources, education and training are provided in the legal framework so that all participants have equal access and understanding. As we approach the millennium, we still await the establishment of a national Forensic Science Institute, a properly financed and provisioned independent scientific facility, a properly indexed and authorised registration system. Despite repeated request from Lord Dainton's Committee, from Lord Taylor the former Lord Chief Justice, and to a limited extent from the Royal Commission, no progress has been made. Even as this book is published, Michael Howard, commenting on the Caddy report into potential semtex contamination, is still not sure whether he should adopt a proposal for an independent inspectorate to maintain quality performance, protocol and standards. This attitude is both arrogant and shamefully little short of criminal. His approach demonstrates a continuing lack of adequate concern for miscarriages of justice and has more to do with his insatiable desire for policies which might win votes and incur little cost.

Following Kevin's conviction, spurred on by his burning sense of injustice, he fought on, persisting in the belief that there must be an expert somewhere in the world who could help.

Despite the allocated time for lodging notices of appeal passing by, the limited letter allowance, the exigencies of the prison library, the difficulties in obtaining transcripts and his own educational background, he sought out and identified the very expertise required. Instead of a consultant paediatrician with pathological experience and a pathologist, called at trial, he consulted the author of the book he had found, a *neuro*surgeon, Mr Wrightson, living in New Zealand. The trial was followed through by direct contact and support from this eminent practitioner and beyond to another expert of great standing, Dr Helen Whitwell – a *neuro*pathologist. Their opinions were in stark contrast to the original opinions.

The decision of the single judge to refuse these new opinions is part of a dangerous wind of change apparent in the Court of Appeal. It was hoped that earlier miscarriage cases had alerted the Court to the deficiencies of science (Maguire, Judith Ward) and the need for special care. It was hoped that the public debate and proposed changes to the terms of the Criminal Appeal Act would lead to a greater willingness to receive fresh evidence. The 'no second bite of the cherry' doctrine is an uncritical and simplistic test which owes more to the desire for finality than a search for truth. It does not even discern whether it is the same cherry.

Kevin's testament is also a monument. Before it is too late, let there be no more names inscribed in the hall of judicial infamy.

Michael Mansfield QC

KEVIN CALLAN'S STORY

CHAPTER

· · · · · · · · · · · · · · · · ·

I

I WAS BORN in 1958 and raised in Gorton, Manchester. I had two elder sisters, Janice and Lynn, and an elder brother, Keith, so I was the baby of the family. As soon as I was old enough, I went to Saint James's school. I will never forget the first day: my mam made me wear a cardigan! I yelled all the way there and for most of the morning. 'Cardigans are for girls, not boys, and I aren't a girl, I'm a boy,' I roared.

I can't remember much about my early childhood, apart from the games we played after school. I couldn't wait to get out of that stuffy classroom and go home to change into my scruffs. Then out I'd go to meet other young kids my age. We'd play Postman's Knock where one of us banged on a door and ran away before anyone could answer it and we'd play football with a can or whatever we could lay our hands on. A real ball was a rarity in those days.

Football has always played a big part in my life and I follow Manchester United to this day. I've never forgotten the European Cup Final in which United played Benfica at Wembley and won 4–1. In those days my dad was trucking up and down the country and had a massive red and white rosette attached to the front of his lorry. I went with him every now and then. I loved those trips, pounding up and down the A roads before there were motorways. The roads were rocky and I was thrown all over the cab. We lived on butties and flasks of tea, an endless round of picnics, which was all part of the fun for me though nothing out of the ordinary for Dad. And there were all those new places where people spoke a weird lingo. Dad went mad at me for laughing when he asked directions from a local. On a trip to Scotland, I once asked him, 'Can you really understand what they're saying?'

'Yes, course I can,' he said.

Liar, I thought. There's no way *anyone* could understand that. He must have done though, because he always got to where he was meant to be going after one of these conversations.

My secondary school was called Varna Street. It was also in Gorton but I liked it much better, partly because they took football more seriously there. I was in the school team and played in goal. I haven't a clue why I chose such a mad position but I enjoyed it all the same. We didn't get too many hammerings, although we endured one 6–0 defeat – and yes, I was in goal!

I was happy at Varna Street, where discipline was strict but fair. I knew everyone there and we were mainly United fans, which suited me just fine. And I met my first girlfriend there. We'd go off snogging under the canal bridge after school and I'd tell my mam and dad that I'd been for football practice in the park.

I used to go to Old Trafford to watch my idols as often as I could: Best, Charlton, Crerrand, Stiles, Stepney and Law were a miracle to watch and it never failed to amaze me how many people could be squeezed into the ground for a match. My bedroom wall was plastered with pictures of my heroes. I kept a scrapbook and an autograph book in which I collected the signatures of every United player. I even achieved my ambition of talking to all the players! I used to 'wag' school to go and watch them train at the Cliffe and it was here that I learnt what football was and was not about. It meant a lot more than just playing your guts out on a Saturday afternoon and being idle for the rest of the week. The training sessions were sheer hard work and the players were put through torture to achieve United's international standard. I watched the goalkeepers with close interest. They were singled out for reflex training in which someone behind them would kick a ball hard at a wall and the goalkeeper would have to 'save' it as it rebounded. The effort they all put in was worth it, though, when you saw the way they played on a Saturday. Then I knew why they trained so hard.

After Varna Street, I went to Wright Robinson High School in Abbey Hey, Gorton, a very strict outfit: if we forgot an item of sports kit we were slippered. The headmaster was a ginger-haired nutter called Bates. It will come as no surprise that we called him Basher Bates. He was lethally accurate with that slipper and his face would go bright red as he went to town on us. My first visit to him was for setting light to a bin in the lads' toilet. I couldn't sit down for the rest of the day and ever afterwards did my best to keep well away from him.

I enjoyed the school, though, and some of the teachers were superb, especially the fellow who took us for History. Every lesson he'd say, 'What do we want? History or a story?' There was no choice really – the story came out on top every time.

I left that school at thirteen or fourteen because my family was moving to Glossop in Derbyshire. It was a whole new start for me and I had to make new friends all over again. Not that that was too difficult as I made friends easily, with both girls and boys. The girls could be a bit choosy, but I soon had one of my own.

Here, again, football was an important part in my life: I played for the school and also managed to get a place in a Sunday league team. I was even being watched by scouts, such was my progress as a goalkeeper but, needless to say, I didn't take up football as a career.

This school was much more easygoing than the ones I'd been to in Gorton and eventually I got rather bored with the laxness. We had sly ciggies in class and if I had the same lesson as my girl we sat at the same long and high desk and got up to God knows what with our hands underneath it. The horror time for the teachers must have been when girls and boys had Cookery together. I loathed this and took to hurling dough and other stuff around the room. It got so bad that the teacher tried to send me to the head. I had other ideas, though: I walked out of school never to return.

It was inevitable that the wagman would pay me and my parents a visit. He threatened us with court action unless I went back but I dug in my toes. He told me I'd have to go to court unless I could give him a good reason for not attending school. 'My reason,' I said, 'is that I don't like it.'

He asked how he could persuade me to go back but after a lot of talk we came up with the notion that perhaps instead I could decorate old people's houses. A week or two later he was back to tell me, much to my surprise, that I could. So this was the way I spent the last year and a half of my schooling. It suited me fine not to have to sit in classrooms listening to the claptrap spewed up by the teachers. I would have carried on but this school was so far behind what I had been doing at my previous school and I couldn't see what good it would do me to repeat all the stuff I'd already done. Hence my boredom.

I went back to school once to meet the careers officer. I didn't have a clue what I wanted to do but leant towards painting and decorating as that was what I'd been doing anyway. I had a bit of luck here and found work straight away with a local firm, which lasted until cars entered my life. Then I looked out for an apprentice mechanic's job and found one more or less straight away. The only snag was that it was in Manchester and I had to travel there daily by bus. It wasn't long, however, before the boss took pity on me and paid for me to have driving lessons. It would benefit both of us if I could drive: I'd be able to attend breakdowns and fetch parts on my own.

I passed my test after seven lessons and my gaffer put me on his insurance and gave me the firm's Morris Minor van. No more bus journeys to work *and* I got to keep it over weekends.

I went all over the show in that van, showing off to my mates. I had passed my test and had a van. I was on top of the world. It didn't last long, though. I pranged the van up a kerb and smashed the suspension. Next morning I tried to get into the garage to repair it before work but failed and instead opted to keep quiet about it.

What a fatal mistake that turned out to be. A call for a breakdown came, of course, and my gaffer got in the van to go out to it. I watched as he went hobbling and bumping up the road. He went berserk – because I hadn't told him rather than because I'd done the damage – and terminated my employment forthwith.

After this I got a job as a driver with a firm who made cardboard and plastics and to start with I enjoyed it immensely, being my own person out on the road. It didn't last, though, and I began to drift from job to job and spent some time out of work.

This was when I got into DJ-ing: I began as a mobile, travelling to many venues doing weddings, parties, Christmas dos and suchlike. It was while I was in this line of work that I had the great good fortune to meet a girl called Les. I was DJ-ing at a local pub in Glossop when this cracker walked in. She was absolutely gorgeous and the best of it was that she was after me just as much as I was after her. We got a thing going and would spend weekends together. I'd sometimes stay at her parents' home and other times we'd stay at her mate's.

But every Saturday morning I was off: Saturdays were strictly for Manchester United games, no matter where they were playing. This, of course, got on Les's nerves, as it does with every woman! After a few months Les and I split up:

someone told her I'd said something that I hadn't and it was many years before Les knew exactly what had been said.

Not long after this I got married for the first time, I don't know why. It didn't last, we got divorced and I moved back into Manchester, where I met, and married, another girl. I must have had a rush of blood to the head to do it again. We had two children, Angela and Scott. I love them to bits and I'm very proud of them too. Sadly, this marriage ended in divorce too, and it began to dawn on me that marriage was probably best left well alone – which fine idea I stuck to until Les re-entered my life.

CHAPTER

2

DURING MY TIME apart from Les, I kept bumping into her but it was while I was trucking in about 1985 that we sorted ourselves out. I was destined for Italy and was heading through Hyde when I saw Les pushing a pram with two children in it. I stopped and asked how she was getting on. She wasn't happy so I asked her outright to come with me to Italy along with the kids. I told her I'd get passports for them and that she wouldn't need any money with me, but she said she couldn't so I went on my way.

Another few months went by during which I thought about nothing but Les. So, when I got back from another trip to Italy I made a promise to myself: I would not go out of the country again until I had found out where she was living and had been to see her. Somehow I got her phone number from directory enquiries and called. When she answered I asked if I could see her. She agreed and what a joy it was to learn that she was living alone. I asked if we could go out together, then if I could stay with her. She said yes. We went out that night and decided straight away to live together.

Les had two daughters: Mandy, three, and Natalie, two. Mandy had cerebral palsy but to me she has always been a normal child – a right little belter, in fact. Because of the condition, she wasn't as able-bodied as other children her age but nothing would deter her from giving anything a go. We soon got a superb relationship going between the four of us. I used to bring the children toys from my European trips and after a while they knew the sound of my truck. When they heard it they would be at the door, waiting to give me a kiss and to see what goodies I'd got them. Natalie was a great kid too, and loved our new surroundings. We became one very happy, close-knit family. I also met Les's parents, who welcomed me as one of their own.

I soon got myself involved with some of the people responsible for Mandy's everyday care and I took a big interest in what was required of parents with a cerebral-palsied child and helped in any way I could, especially to exercise her. Les and I soon realised that Mandy had come on in leaps and bounds since I had moved in. I had got her out of nappies and off the bottle, taught her how to use a knife and fork, how to get up the stairs on her own, etc. I knew she could achieve a lot as long as we could keep up her determination to overcome her disability. I soon began to teach her to walk. She wore leg splints with special boots and a splint on her left hand, which otherwise was constantly clenched. I couldn't get enough of the children and Les, I loved them so much.

One day I was walking Mandy up and down the kitchen. Suddenly, and very gently, I let go of her. To my delight, she carried on walking alone. I bellowed for Les to come quickly and when she got to me I showed her what Mandy could do. The tears filled our eyes as we watched. It was the first major breakthrough.

The next came with letter cards designed to improve her lip movement and speech. Here, we had lots of fun. It was hard work but when Mandy blurted out, 'A' followed by 'Apple' it was all worth it. When we moved on to B which was shown with a banana, it took a while for her to grasp the word and it kept coming out as 'nana'. We laughed our heads off and she got it in the end – and, gradually, the rest of the alphabet.

While we were making headway with both Mandy's and Natalie's education Les and I had been planning our wedding to take place in October 1990. We saw the vicar and sent out the invitations but had to put it off because my workload at the time was too heavy to allow me to take time off for it.

That year the four of us went on holiday to my parents' home in Colwyn Bay, North Wales. My mother, Joan, and father, Arthur, took to the children and the holiday went like a dream for the kids. At the Sun Centre in Rhyl there was a slide into the water and I'd take Mandy to the top and come sliding down with her. The children loved the funfair and they went on most of the little ones' rides, roundabouts and minicars. I had never known before how simple it was to give children so much excitement and joy and I felt tremendously fulfilled.

However, I will never forget Les asking me to go on some object that looked like a boat and swung violently to and fro. I studied it for a while and noticed that the people already on board weren't looking very well, but I allowed myself to be talked into getting on it. Les assured me that I would be perfectly all right. Liar, I thought, and off it went. It wasn't too bad to start with but then my insides went into orbit. I grabbed hold of Les for dear life, but all she could do was laugh her head off at me. I went all colours and when the operator of the ride saw how I felt he made his contraption go even faster. Eventually it stopped. I felt dreadful and my body took its time getting back to normal. Later, Les said casually, 'Do you fancy going on that ride again?' At least I was able to laugh!

We didn't want this holiday to end but eventually we had to

go home. At least we would see my parents regularly as they came to our home whenever they were in the area, bringing something for the children on every visit.

A few months later, Les and I went to Portugal on one of my trips. We left the children in the capable care of one of her friends. I had to go to Lisbon and Benfica and although we had problems at Customs on the Spanish/Portuguese border, we enjoyed the drive down. Just before we set off on the journey home we telephoned Les's parents to make sure that all was well at home, to discover that Mandy had been taken to hospital. I mad-rushed back to the UK where we broke down with engine failure. I telephoned my brother, Keith, to collect us, which he did.

When we got home we found out that Mandy's problem had been a mild attack of gastroenteritis. Les called the hospital and was told that it had been nothing serious, that it wouldn't pose a long-term threat to Mandy's health and that there was no need to worry. We had been frightened to death, of course, but Mandy made a full recovery. We agreed that Les would not come with me on any further trips because we couldn't bear the thought of something happening to one of the children when neither of us was around.

Shortly after that, we decided to go to live in Wales, near my parents. It was close enough to Manchester to see Les's family and there was a special school for Mandy and a nursery for Natalie. I could work from anywhere in the UK as my job took me all over the country anyway.

I got to meet some of the professionals involved with Mandy on a regular basis. The health visitor brought about my first active part in Mandy's routine and then I met the physiotherapist, who taught me how to exercise Mandy's limbs and muscles properly. It seemed cruel to me, the way her legs, head, arms and every part of her body were being pulled and twisted this way and that. But there was not a murmur of protest from Mandy during the ordeals. I was frightened of hurting her when I started but when we got going Mandy took to the exercises well. She had her own way of making me understand when she'd had enough: she would say 'Keg', and then 'Plant pot'.

A sponge roll was allotted to Mandy, courtesy of the CDU (Child Development Unit), to help exercise her legs and arms by rolling her over but without letting her fall. In practice it didn't work out like this. I pushed her gently to and fro until she was able to do it herself. To begin with, she would go head first over the roll and end up flat out in an untidy heap. It was great fun, this teaching lark, but it was also a serious method of training for Mandy. Soon she learnt that putting her hands out in front of her stopped her falling off and that she could use her feet to stop her ending up on her bum. The point of the exercise was to use her legs and arms to build up her muscles, and as Mandy enjoyed doing this she got a lot of benefit from it.

Eventually she was able to sit astride the roll and watch telly from it. Until, that is, Natalie pushed her off! Mandy was nothing short of brilliant in her own special ways. She would often pounce on me and use me as a rocking horse. There were colour charts too and beads for her to count, and we had a lot of fun with those also. With the beads Mandy could soon count to ten and the colour charts helped her to recognise different colours. Drawing and writing came next. The pride and joy that I felt in Mandy are impossible to put into words, but I still have that same pride today and my memories are mine for ever.

The whole family got a shock in November 1990 when Mandy returned from her special school, Poplar Street Nursery, with a big bruise on her bottom. I got Les to take her to the GP the following morning, who said it looked like Mandy had fallen on something sharp, possibly a toy. Later that day, Les contacted the health visitor and they went together to Mandy's school to find out what had happened.

They were told that as no one at the school had seen the accident happen it couldn't have taken place there.

A few days later, there was another incident. Mandy was at school, standing near one of her nurses/teachers, when another child distracted the attention of the nurse and Mandy fell on to the corner of a table and was cut so severely that she had to be taken to hospital where she had two stitches in a '2 cm deep laceration to the crown of the head'. Immediately afterwards Mandy was sent straight back to school without any X-rays, CT scan tests, or observation being carried out.

When Les and I found out about this accident we contacted the school and told them that Les would collect her straight away. The school was hesitant about letting her go but Les insisted. When they got home it was clear to me that Mandy was very shaken. She was pale and we laid her down on the sofa.

Over the next days and weeks Mandy began to show symptoms that caused Les and me serious concern. She was being sick a lot and especially at night, which was the worst time. She couldn't turn over fast enough to avoid choking on her vomit. I saved her life more than once. One night I found her choking, and I had to lay her over my knees and bang her back to get the vomit out of her lungs.

All the professionals involved with Mandy were personally notified of her symptoms. Les and I stressed how worried we were as it became ever clearer that Mandy needed attention. Her eyes were sunken, she was white and not eating normally. She was always tired and didn't want to do most things. Temper tantrums developed and she often pointed to her head and stomach. Her hair fell out and she lost weight. Finally, Mandy was seen by the CDU and Les and I saw a paediatrician on 14 December 1990. We told him all about Mandy's symptoms and how worried we were and I also said that the stitches in Mandy's head were causing her pain because they pulled on her scalp. His reply was Mandy's symptoms stemmed from her frustration at not being able to do the things she wanted to do and that the stitches would dissolve in their own time.

I asked him to explain what cerebral palsy was. He drew diagrams of the brain and said that part of the brain was dead. I again expressed my concern that Mandy's recent symptoms had only developed since her fall at school.

While at the CDU Mandy was also examined by a speech therapist, who noted that she was dribbling, and concluded that she showed evidence of having a motor speech problem. She was also seen by a physiotherapist and by someone about her eyes, who told us that Mandy had developed a squint: she would need to wear glasses. No connection was made between the squint and the serious fall at school, the importance of which will become clear later.

When we left the CDU, Les and I felt frustrated in that we still had exactly the same problems as we had gone in with. Even worse was the fact that no expert or specialist advice had been given to us as responsible parents. Our worry deepened as Mandy got no better.

We spent Christmas 1990 quietly at home and wondered what the new year held for us. Les began the year with health problems of her own and Mandy was no better. I was trying hard to keep my work going but I felt that someone somewhere had to take note of the gradual deterioration in Mandy's health. No matter who we turned to the answer was always the same: don't worry. I, however, was more than worried now because Mandy was being totally ignored by the doctors. It was impossible to believe that so many professional people could fail to take suitable steps to stop such a serious decline in a child's health. I kept hearing the same unanswered question over and over again in my head: why, why, *why* won't they do something?

It came as a great relief to me when I was laid off work in mid-February 1991. Work was the least of my concerns.

Mandy had long been the top priority in my life. From now on Les and I talked to anyone and everyone involved with Mandy. All her symptoms had been reported in her day-school correspondence book with little reaction from the teachers and finally Les took her back to hospital in March. She reiterated all the symptoms again, as well as our deep frustration at the inaction of the medical profession. She got them to agree that Mandy should see the paediatrician who had examined her before, who said that we should bring her in for two days of tests on 27 March. Les had to go in too on that day for a minor gynaecological operation. I felt that, at last, something positive was about to be done. How wrong I was.

Just before they both went into hospital, I told the health visitor all my worries about Mandy's symptoms and also how difficult it was to be totally responsible for saving Mandy's life at night when she was choking on her vomit. There were professional people to deal with these problems and I wanted them to do just that.

The twenty-seventh of March arrived and Les and Mandy went into Tameside General Hospital. I stayed at home with Natalie, but went to see Les after her operation. She was in some pain but the staff from the children's ward had been to see her and asked that she go and tend to Mandy because the staff down there had difficulty calming her. I was horrified. Les had just had an operation and yet the staff wanted her to do their job. I was rapidly losing any hope of success as far as Mandy's immediate progress was concerned.

After two days, Les and Mandy came home. Les told me that Mandy had had no tests. I couldn't believe what I was hearing. I told Les that we were going to take Mandy straight up to the CDU and get them to sort the mess.

It was Les who went to the CDU, only to be told that they could say nothing because Mandy had only just come out of hospital and they didn't as yet have any record of her admission. The following week Les had a letter from Tameside

General Hospital telling Les that she could have been pregnant at the time of her operation. She would now need another to remove what may have been our unborn child. Les broke down and cried in my arms.

We considered taking legal action against the hospital for not carrying out proper tests to determine whether Les was pregnant before her operation.

April came, and I had a conversation with Mandy's physiotherapist and told her how bad things were getting. All our relations were saying how unwell she looked – actually, she looked worse than at any time since I had known and loved her.

Sometime over the weekend of 5–7 April, I had Mandy sitting on the kitchen worktop washing the pots with me. Natalie was watching television. All of a sudden there was a loud cacophony of sound from the living room which made Mandy and me jump. I ran in and found Natalie standing in front of the television with the remote control: she had turned the volume right up to full belt and she didn't know whether to laugh or cry. I took the control from her and turned the volume down. Then Mandy shouted so I ran back into the kitchen. She was lying on the floor and as I went to pick her up I saw blood around her head. She had fallen off the worktop, hit her head and the cut from November had reopened. And not for the first time. She was also bruised right down one side of her body, from her face to her leg. It seemed obvious to me that she had caught herself as she fell. I made sure that she wasn't seriously hurt and we carried on washing the pots together.

On Monday, 8 April, I got both children up and gave them their breakfast. I got Mandy ready for school and we waited for the taxi to arrive. After she went, I got Natalie ready and made Les a brew. Around eleven a car drew up outside our home and through the window we saw Mandy being carried to the front door. We were told that she had been brought home because she was not well. How observant of them to notice, for once.

In the late afternoon I, too, was feeling ill and went to bed. A short time later two people turned up, introduced themselves to Les as social workers and asked for the children to be taken to our local clinic for a medical examination. There, they were examined by a Dr Marie Lawrence, who stated that the injuries to Mandy were consistent with the fall from the worktop and caused her no concern. However, when Les got home with the girls, she was upset: it struck us both as odd that social workers should want the children clinically examined when the overriding problems concerned Mandy's health. We realised that we were under scrutiny and could only conclude that someone's twisted mind was looking elsewhere for reasons behind Mandy's ill health.

Mandy went to school on Tuesday and Wednesday. On Wednesday night Les and I stayed up until the early hours of Thursday morning talking about Mandy's health problems and how those people had turned up out of the blue wanting the children clinically examined. What would happen next, we wondered, and what would be the best way forward? Les asked me what I would do if my children were being treated in the way Tameside Hospital and the authorities were treating hers. I told her that I would immediately get the children's own GP out to examine them at home. I hoped she would get Mandy and Natalie's doctor to examine them at home.

On the Thursday morning Les called out Mandy's GP, Dr Susan McClure. She arrived in the latter part of the afternoon while I was out. Les told her that all Mandy's symptoms were still evident. All Dr McClure did was look in Mandy's ears and say that she was fine.

We kept Mandy off school on Friday so we could keep a close watch on her, the situation was now so serious. She walked up and down the front garden path with the aid of her leg splints, special boots, hand splint and walking frame and she had on her glasses. Even so, she had a bad fall which made her cry when her frame toppled over and she banged her head on one of the paving slabs. We took her indoors where I rubbed butter into the nasty bump on her head. After lots of cuddling she eventually calmed down.

It was Mandy's fourth birthday on Sunday, 14 April 1991. We set a little party up for her and Natalie with sandwiches and a cake. My parents came and Les's brother, sister-in-law and their son. Mam and Dad brought along a lady with whom we were to exchange houses in Wales. She had a look round our place and was impressed with what she saw, so we made the final arrangements to go ahead. The children were told that we were going to live by the seaside and were more than excited. The party went well, with Mandy opening her presents. Afterwards I began to make a cardboard model of a pram for Mandy. It was supposed to be one that a child could do but I had problems with it and couldn't see how any child could have put it together. It was really special, making this model up, because Mandy stuck like glue to my side, watching every move I made. It took two or three hours to finish it but the effort was worthwhile: when I gave it to Mandy she was thrilled. I think she saw the struggle I had had to make it for her because she would not let go of it for a long time after I gave it to her.

Inevitably, Natalie decided that *she* wanted a pram too and that the short cut to getting one was to pinch Mandy's. All hell broke loose as they began to fight over it. We explained to Natalie that the pram was part of Mandy's birthday and things settled down.

When bedtime arrived I got Mandy ready and took her up, to her own room. She was on her potty and I had one last game with her before I put her into bed and gave her a kiss goodnight. I got her to hold her forefinger up and slowly guide it to the tip of my nose. 'Right, Mandy,' I said, 'watch my eyes.' When she saw them cross she burst out laughing. By now Les had come up and was watching us and she, too, had a good laugh.

The following day Les was due back in hospital so they could patch up the mess they'd made. We got up around five to get her ready. Her father was taking her in. Both children woke up while we were moving about the house and wanted to come down but it was much too early for them.

Les's father arrived and I kissed her and wished her luck, then began to get the children's breakfast. At around seven-thirty I went to get Natalie up – I got her up first so that both children would not be on the stairs at the same time, which I thought would be dangerous as one could fall and bring the other down with her. When Natalie was downstairs, I got Mandy up, I emptied her potty and went back down, leaving her to make her own way.

I got on with making breakfast until I heard a thud come from the direction of the stairs. When I got there I found Mandy lying at the bottom, saying, 'Fall, fall.' She seemed none the worse, though, got up and had breakfast. Afterwards I got her ready for the taxi to collect her and take her to school.

By about nine no taxi had arrived so I told Mandy that she would not be going to school but instead we would all make a crazy-paving path down the middle of the back garden. I wanted to lay a solid path to the play area which would make Mandy's access to it safer and easier. Both children helped me move the earth in their toy buggies. It was good exercise for Mandy as it meant that she would be standing up while push-ing her buggy to where the earth was tipped out. They also played on the swing and slide. When they were doing this they often fought and slid into each other deliberately so I separated them, putting one on the swing and the other on the slide! By around eleven, after all this activity, Mandy was worn out and asked for a lie-down. I took her up to her bedroom for a sleep.

Around eleven-thirty our health visitor called and asked why Mandy was not at school. I told her that the taxi had not turned up. She said, 'Well, didn't you phone for one?' I asked her what she meant and she explained that when a child is not in school on the previous day, the taxi has to be rebooked. I told her that I didn't even know the taxi's phone number, never mind that I had to rebook it, and that Les was back in hospital. I said that Mandy was having a lie-down and showed her the back garden. She was impressed but asked if I would lower the approach to the play area as it was a bit steep.

'No problem,' I said. I showed her some clothes-peg models that I had made with the children and the cardboard pram. She asked if I would like her to take Mandy to school but I told her that it would not be worth it because Mandy would be asleep until dinner. Also, I was going to take both children to see their mother if she wasn't coming out of hospital that day. After about fifteen minutes the health visitor left.

After dinner we all went back into the garden but somewhere around one o'clock a lady called, saying that she had something to do with the school. I had never seen her before. She asked for Les but when I told her Les was in hospital she left an appointment for Les. Around three a friend came to give me £5 from Les's mother. He didn't stay long; he was taking his dog to the vet for some injections.

Back to the path I went, with the children playing happily. Mandy was on the slide with Natalie on the swing. She was trying to walk up it instead of using the steps as I had taught her the previous year. I was worried that she might fall so I taught her how to use the steps again. She soon got the hang of it and it was funny to watch her go down the slide. She could only go down head first because of her mobility difficulties. When she got to the bottom there was a little drop from the slide end to the grass and every time she got there she would laugh her little head off as she flopped on to the grass.

A bit later on we were all thirsty so I went in to make us some tea. While I was in the kitchen I heard Mandy shout for me so I ran out to find her at the bottom of the slide's steps. Her glasses had come off and there was a mark at the side of her left eye with some scratches round it. I made sure she was all right then took her glasses indoors and she went back to playing in the garden.

She was on her knees, pushing the swing to and fro, when Les arrived back from the hospital. I kissed Les and started to tell her about all the day's events: the falls that Mandy had had and the people who had called, that no taxi had arrived to collect Mandy for school. She said, 'What do you mean? I ordered a cab from the hospital this morning.' She seemed groggy from the anaesthetic so I asked her if she'd like a brew and told her to sit on the bench near the back door, where she could see the children.

They wanted a drink, too, and while the kettle was boiling, I said to Les, 'Watch this,' and I put Mandy on the swing, pushing her quite high. I pretended that she was kicking me as she was coming down and she was squeaking with laughter. I went in to get the tea and left Les to watch the children.

Suddenly, she shouted, 'Kev! Quick! Get her off the swing! She's gone white.' I rushed out to Mandy and she was like a ghost. I brought her up to the back door and her eyes were glazed over. She began to cry and point to her head and belly. We asked her if it hurt and she said it did. She pointed to her head and belly again and said she was tired. I gave the children their drinks and Mandy gulped hers. She was crying again so we decided that she could lie down until we got some food sorted out. A chippy tea would make things easier all round so I told Les I'd go and get it while she would be better sitting down. She, however, was determined to go and said that she wanted some other bits from the other shops.

While Les was out, I tidied, washed up and vacuumed. Then I got Mandy's all-in-one suit out of the kitchen cupboard and went to get her ready for bed. I did not want Les doing a single thing and I wanted to get as much done as possible while she was at the shops. I put Mandy's suit on her in her bedroom and was waiting for her to come after me. As she had already fallen down the stairs that day I was going to walk down with her. As she was coming out of her room she suddenly stopped on her knees and vomited ferociously. She began to struggle for air so I yanked her up off the floor, ran with her into the bathroom, tipped her over the toilet and started banging her back. I felt her go limp so I laid her on the floor, pushed on her belly and chest and blew into her mouth. For some reason, I got a jug of water and wet her head. I took off her all-in-one suit and carried on pushing and blowing. There was sick all over the place leading from her room into the bathroom.

I felt panic grip me. What am I supposed to fucking do? I thought. For God's sake, help me someone. 'Les, Les, help me,' I shouted.

From nowhere she came running up the stairs and into the bathroom. I yelled, 'I don't know what to do. Go next door and phone for a fucking ambulance, quick!' I carried on with what I was doing and was suddenly joined by our neighbour, Margaret, who joined in. As I was pushing Mandy's belly and chest I pulled a big blob of something out of her mouth and she made a gurgling noise. I'm getting her breathing, I thought.

Les was screaming at the top of the stairs and she pulled the banister off the wall in her own panic.

A medic came running up to the bathroom and I told him, 'I don't know what to do.'

He said, 'Carry on, mate, you're doing a good job,' so I did while he took something out of a sealed packet, placed it in Mandy's mouth and took over from me. He called to his assistant, 'Quick! I need a suction unit. The airway's blocked.' It arrived and he said, 'It's OK, I've cleared it.'

In the ambulance a medic cut off Mandy's vest and put two round things on her chest with a mask over her mouth. She was attached to a monitor just above her head and I saw traces of what I took to be a heartbeat.

The two medics didn't know which hospital we were going to. Here we were, in a life-and-death situation, and they didn't have a clue where to go!

We ended up at the dreaded Tameside Hospital.

The ambulance doors were flung open and Mandy was gone in a flash. Les and I followed, to be taken to a room down the corridor where they had just taken Mandy. We were offered tea and the telephone. We called Les's parents, who were soon with us. Her dad Neville's immediate reaction was, 'This all started as a result of that bleeding fall at school last year.' Peg, her mum, went into the room with Les and I stayed with Neville. I told him about all the day's events and how it was that Mandy had been rushed into hospital.

I asked anyone who appeared to be anything resembling a doctor for news. Eventually, I went in to Les and wrapped my arms around her. We held each other tightly. Then, back to the corridor I went where the pacing-up-and-down syndrome got hold of me.

Someone came towards Neville and me saying, 'I'm sorry, she's dead.'

Neville said simply, 'Oh, shit.' I ran at a wall. Maybe this was my inner self reacting to how we had been banging our heads against a brick wall for the past six months. I went back to the doctor and Neville asked him why Mandy had died.

He said, 'A brain haemorrhage. She wouldn't have known a thing.'

Neville asked if any tests were done in November but the doctor said, 'Not as far as I am aware.' When he was asked if any tests had been carried out in March that year, he replied, 'Not as far as I am aware.' Neville was getting angry. He asked the doctor to produce Mandy's medical records. 'I don't know where they are,' was the response.

I saw the immediate danger of this reply, and took Neville away before he could take out his frustration on the doctor who could hardly be held responsible. I said to him, 'Leave it for the court, because we'll sue them for what they've done.' These words were soon to be turned upside down. Then I went to Les and held her tightly. We both wept in sheer disbelief of all that had happened in these last few minutes.

CHAPTER

·················

3

WE WERE ALLOWED a private ten minutes or so alone with Mandy in a side room. She looked just as though she was sleeping and would wake up at any moment. We both touched and stroked her, willing her to wake up. Les kept saying, 'My baby, my baby.'

This is all so unreal, I thought. I was called out of the room and asked for a nurse to look after Les. I couldn't bear to think how she must have been feeling. Only this morning she had had an operation in this hospital and now she was holding Mandy's lifeless body.

A nurse went to Les and took Mandy from her. Les was laid on a bed and given a sedative to ease the shock.

Two plain-clothes policemen wanted to have a word with me. We went to the end of the corridor where I told them of everything that had happened over the last six months. I began with the fall at school in November 1990, ending with that day's events. I noticed that the policemen were not writing down all that I was telling them. They were simply jotting down bits of my words. Therefore the whole story was not written down and when it was read out in court it did not sound like the story I had told them.

Would I take them back to our home? they asked. 'Of course,' I replied. I went to Les and told her I would see her back at home with her parents. She didn't want me to go but I told her that she would soon be home and to relax and allow the medication to take effect.

Off we went to our home, the three of us. On the way there the car stopped at a phone box and one policeman made a call. When we arrived at our house I showed them the layout. Beginning with the upstairs rooms, I showed them Mandy's bedroom – the trail of vomit still led from it to the bathroom. I couldn't go into the bathroom but saw Mandy's all-in-one suit on the floor with the jug partly full of water. Then we went downstairs to find a photographer there. He had appeared from nowhere and without my consent or knowledge. We went out to the back garden where more photographs were taken. Then it was back to the living room. Les and her parents arrived and I put my arms around Les and held her as we both cried with numbness and sheer shock.

Natalie was brought back from our neighbours' home and was put to bed as it was getting late. Shortly afterwards the policemen and Les's parents went home too, saying that they would be back in the morning.

There was no way I could go near the bathroom so Les had to clear it up. I told her that I had almost kept Mandy with us because I had heard her gurgling and that I felt such a failure for not being able to keep her alive, as I had done before. I said that if I had had first-aid training then maybe things would have been a bit different and Mandy would still be here. Les reassured me and held me close, telling me that I couldn't have done any more to keep Mandy alive. A while later she went for a bath and called me to her. I went up to the bathroom but couldn't bring myself to go in so stood outside.

Sometime later a friend called round. I broke the news of Mandy's death to him. I kept breaking down as I went over what had happened. Eventually, he left and we were alone for the rest of the night. We did our best to get some sleep, which was close on impossible, but I must have drifted off at some stage. I woke to find that Les was not at my side. I immediately knew where she would be and went to Mandy's bedroom. She was sitting on Mandy's bed, holding Mandy's favourite teddy and crying, rocking to and fro. She was totally enveloped in her grief. We cried together for a while, then I managed to get her to come down and made her some tea. Miraculously we managed some sleep, to wake in the morning to our own nightmare.

Another day had dawned but this was so different from any other. It was so empty and hollow, 16 April 1991, the day after our special darling had lost her fight for life. We made no plans for the day and got on with doing the washing. Natalie had no idea that her elder sister had tragically died. How she would cope with the news only time would tell.

During the morning Neville and Peg came round with their other daughter, Sue. Later we all went to their home. When we got there, I phoned my parents to tell them about Mandy. Les came upstairs to make the call with me as I couldn't do it on my own. I dialled the number and my mother, Joan, answered. Only tears came out, accompanied by the word 'Mam'. She asked me what the matter was but I couldn't speak properly. Les held me really tight and tried to help me in the way I had helped her the day before. 'Mam,' I said, 'it's Mandy.'

'What about Mandy?' she asked.

'She's . . .' and that was all I could say. I tried again. 'Mam, Mandy is no longer with us.'

'Oh, shit, Jesus Christ,' she said.

I managed to tell her briefly what had happened the day before and at the hospital. I told her that I wanted to be with

Mandy because I felt I should have saved her. My mother shouted for my father, Arthur, and told him. They were both deeply shocked as they loved her too.

I told my mam that I would keep her informed, adding that Les, Natalie and myself would like to spend some time with them once we were sorted out. I needed some of my own family around me just as Les needed hers at this time. Mam said she'd arrange transport for us to her home and I said I'd call again as soon as I could make definite plans.

We were waiting for a call from the police, so that Les and her parents could formally identify Mandy at Tameside Hospital, and we contacted Mandy's natural father to tell him that we would all meet at Les's and my home later in the day with the undertakers to arrange the funeral.

The call for the identification procedure finally came and Les and her parents went off to the hospital. Sue, Natalie and I were going back to our home so that someone would be there when Mandy's father and the undertakers arrived. I told Les I'd see her later and we set off in Sue's car where I had Natalie sitting with me. I held her tight and kept breaking down. Once home I showed Sue the note that had been left the day before by the woman who asked for Les. We agreed to throw it away so Les wouldn't have to suffer even more distress.

A while later, Les and her parents got home. Les came into my arms and I broke down again, telling her how proud of her I was for having done the unthinkable and identified her own daughter's body. We talked about Natalie, Les and me going to my parents' for a few days. Neville and Peg thought it a good idea but first we had to make the funeral arrangements. I phoned my parents, who said my brother Keith would collect us around seven, which would give us ample time to sort things out.

When Mandy's father arrived, I told him that he and Les must travel in the same car for the funeral. All through that day I was wondering how Natalie was managing to function properly with all this heartbreak around her. This world can be very cruel to the young.

When the undertakers arrived I was in the kitchen, ironing. Two men came in to me and asked if they could talk to me. I said, 'Yes, of course you can,' and we went into the kitchen. They introduced themselves as DCI Walker and DC Stamper from Stalybridge police station.

Walker wasted no time. 'I'm not satisfied with your explanation and I am arresting you on suspicion of murder.'

I slithered down the kitchen cupboard, which I was leaning against, to the floor. What fucking explanation did he mean? I asked myself. I'd never seen these two in my life, never mind made any explanation to them. I managed to get up and got a drink of water.

'Come on,' they said, and grabbed my arm. They took me through to the living room, where Les was sitting on the sofa, crying her eyes out, with a WPC at her side.

I bent down to her and said, 'What's happening, babba?' but before she could say anything I was pulled away and taken outside where there was an armada of police cars, marked and unmarked. I was put into the back of a blue car and the nightmare took a sick twist.

So many codes and locks, accompanied by massive shutters and doors. All this just to get into a police station where I was suddenly standing at a desk. My thoughts turned to the many recent and notorious miscarriages of justice. I hoped and prayed that I was not going to be the victim of another. I knew how the Birmingham Six, the Guildford Four and the Maguire Seven had felt at the moment of arrival in a police station. So many people in uniforms were staring at me and I was frightened. None of it made sense to me. I had done nothing wrong to deserve being here.

'Empty your pockets,' someone said. I gave them my tobacco and lighter, which were logged on a large piece of paper and not returned to me. 'Do you want a solicitor?' I was asked.

'Do I need one?' I replied. They said it was up to me. I asked to make a call to my parents so that they could arrange for the family solicitor to see me. Then I was put in a hole in the wall, which they called a cell. It stank of urine and excrement and had white-tiled walls covered in graffiti.

A while later I was told I could call my parents. I dialled their number. Mam answered. 'Mam,' I said, 'I've been arrested on suspicion of murder. Would you please get a solicitor to Stalybridge for me?'

'Jesus Christ,' she said, and was then dumbstruck.

The following day a solicitor, Mr Hudson, arrived and I told him I'd done nothing wrong. He said, 'I know, they're clutching at straws.' He gave me a cigarette and we went into a room where Walker and Stamper were sitting behind a desk with a tape recorder on it. According to these two cops, this was to be an interview. They went through the formalities and then it was on with the show.

I told them everything that had happened in Mandy's life since the fall at school in November 1990, right up to 15 April 1991, the day of her death. I broke down several times. To begin with, the two cops were being very ordinary with me. Then, after a while, they began to hammer their true feelings through to me.

First I was asked to describe certain falls that Mandy had had. I did so in the best possible manner I could. I began by answering their questions about the November fall at Mandy's school. They did not want to know that no X-rays, tests or observation were carried out. Many months later, I found out why this was so.

I answered their questions about the falls on 15 April 1991. Walker told me that I had refused to allow the lady from school to come into our house. I said that she did not ask to come in and that the conversation with her had been limited as I had never seen her before. They went backwards and forwards in what I now believe was a deliberate attempt to confuse me, as if I were not already traumatised enough.

Stamper told me that I did not want Mandy to go to school on the Thursday or Friday of the week before she died because she was covered in bruises and that I was hiding something. I told him that that was not true. Again and again he repeated his allegation. I could almost feel his and Walker's annoyance at my unwavering and truthful replies.

Walker read part of the paediatrician's statement to me: 'Amanda's body bore a large number of injuries, which were consistent with serious physical abuse on several different occasions during the previous week. The assaults involved, in my opinion, shaking and punching.'

Stamper jumped in again. 'The body is black and blue. It's covered in bruises. There isn't a limb, there isn't an area that hasn't got bruises on it. They're not little bruises, they're not bumps and knocks, they're finger prods, they're punch marks, they're big bruises, they're little bruises. They are caused by abuse, that is punching, hitting, kicking, shaking. In the opinion of the Home Office pathologist likewise. Two experienced, qualified doctors in their particular fields have said that is how those injuries have been caused. There's no other explanation.'

Then they jumped back in time to Mandy's schooling. Stamper told me that Mandy didn't want to come home from school and that there had been a marked difference in her over the summer holidays. He told me that Mandy's change in behaviour was because I had moved in with Les.

They said that Mandy had been a troublesome child, that she threw tantrums and always needed attention, that she was like a baby. 'Do you ever lose your temper with her?' I was asked. I told them that I did not but that I got frustrated at times.

Immediately Walker opened up with his barrage of sick accusations. 'Frustrated enough on Monday to shake her and punch her,' he said. I told him no, I had given Mandy her breakfast on Monday and that everything had been like any other normal day. Then he said, 'I didn't say that. I said frustrated enough to shake her and punch her on Monday.' Not at all, I replied.

He said, 'I think that's what happened. The Home Office pathologist has said that the brain injury had been caused by violent shaking and the—' he was saying, but Stamper cut him off.

'There's no other explanation. There's no other way that the injury that caused her death could have been caused other than by vigorous and deliberate shaking of that child. Not just shaking, "Stop it, eat your tea." We're talking about vigorous and violent shaking to such an extent that her brain had gone from side to side within the skull, which caused an injury which subsequently, after a small period of time, caused her to become unconscious and die.'

I said, 'No, I didn't shake her up like that.'

Stamper said, 'No other injury would have presented itself in that way. Falling off the slide, falling down the stairs, a bang on the head wouldn't have presented itself in that way. This is an unusual injury which could only be caused by somebody doing what I just described to you, so if you haven't done it, who has? Nobody, because that child has been in your custody and control.'

I tried to say something but was immediately cut off. They had no interest in anything but trying to get me to admit to something which I had not done. Walker continued, 'You shook her, possibly lost your temper, and that's what caused her to die.'

'I didn't lose my temper,' I said.

Walker was off on a series of unstoppable questions, all of which I did my best to answer. However, he said finally, 'I'm not happy with the explanation that you give and I'm telling you that you are going to be charged with an offence of murder. Do you understand?' He seemed almost joyful.

I do not have a clue what explanation he was basing his accusations on, as he wouldn't let me answer most of what he was asking me. During the tirade my solicitor had sat silent, failing to stop the direct accusations against me.

I was taken to a desk where I was charged with murder, just as Walker had promised. 'Not guilty,' I replied.

I was taken back to a cell and left alone to wonder what had just gone on in that so-called interview. Nothing made an ounce of sense.

CHAPTER

·················

4

A DAY OR so later I was brought before three magistrates at Dukinfield Court. They could easily hear how badly the police wanted me held in custody and they agreed readily. I was in a complete daze. It was quite obvious to me that if the police looked at the true facts surrounding Mandy's death they would have to accept my explanation, but because they did not it became more than clear to me that they were happy to allow a miscarriage of justice to take place – and even substantially contribute to it.

After this hearing, I was taken back to Stalybridge police station and returned to a cell. A young cop stuck his head to the flap in the door and said, 'What have you done her in for?'

I knew then that the police were going to make something out of me.

A short article appeared in our local newspaper, the *Advertiser*, saying that 'a man was helping police with their enquiries'. I was not helping police with their enquiries, I was being subjected to a non-stop barrage of disgusting accusations during which they were trying to force me to admit to something which was not true.

Les had also been taken to Stalybridge to be 'interviewed'. It seems that they wanted to turn her against me by trying to shock her with the murder charge, but Les told them that she could not fault me with either herself or the children. She said that she had never known a lad to have so much patience. Obviously they did not want to hear this.

She went over Mandy's health problems since the fall at school in November 1990 and told them of all the times we had tried to get help for her. 'We'll come to that later,' they said to her. But they did not.

Instead they tried to get her to say that I was violent. 'That fella [me] has shaken, punched, kicked and murdered your kid,' they blasted at her. They hammered at her what the paediatrician and pathologist had reported.

The paediatrician was a Dr Jeffrey Freeman from Tameside General Hospital, the hospital we dreaded because of our previous experiences there. The pathologist was Dr Geoffrey Garrett. Freeman even said that nothing had been done with Mandy on any occasion that she had been in his hospital. I knew nothing about the pathologist except that he had got it all so grossly wrong.

Les also told the police that Mandy's health had gone downhill only since the fall at school. She explained that I had been trying to resuscitate Mandy in the bathroom – which may have caused some of the bruising. She also pointed out that Mandy had been examined on 8 April 1991 by Dr Lawrence, who had actually made a report stating that the injuries to Mandy were consistent with the fall off the kitchen worktop and that any injury had not been caused by abuse – an important statement, as will be seen later.

Again, as in my interview, the police were determined to show Les that they were going to make sure that they brought a case against me, no matter what they were told by her.

Sergeant Smith was interviewing Les. He said to her, a woman who had just lost her little girl, that 'Your little girl has been shaken violently, which has caused her brain to haemorrhage, and her liver is damaged. It's caused by nothing else but a thump, so we've got to assume that Kevin has lost his temper with her, haven't we,' he told Les. 'Kevin has done something, Kevin has lost his temper, lost patience, done something and has shaken and thumped Amanda,' he repeated.

But Les said, 'The patience he's got is unbelievable. He's brilliant with 'em. Even the neighbours and everybody will tell you the same. He's brilliant.' She told him that Mandy was normally covered in bruises because when she was play-ing in the back garden she had no splints on, which made falls all the more frequent with the inevitable bumps and marks on her body. She told him that I had never laid a finger on the children or herself.

He reiterated what the paediatrician had said, but Les reminded him of Dr Lawrence's statement. Smith did not want to hear about Dr Lawrence.

'Don't sit there protecting that fella,' he blasted at Les. 'Something's been going on and we need to know. Somebody has been battering Amanda,' he said again.

Later on in her interview, Les gave the police a piece of vital information. 'When she banged her head at school and she had them stitches, they brought her to the hospital and they didn't give her any X-rays. But I only found out that when my dad phoned up the school, Tuesday morning, and he spoke to the woman who took Mandy to the hospital. He asked was any X-rays done and she says no they just stitched her up and that was it. She just come home but from then on she just didn't seem the same.'

This was not explored during the case and its importance will become horrifyingly clear later.

At the end of her interview Les asked to see me. Smith replied, 'You'll not be seeing him for quite a while.'

*

After a few days on remand at Stalybridge I was told that I was being moved to the Bridewell, Liverpool. I was taken to the charge desk in the police station and checked my property. Two cops were there: they were my escort – I detected their Liverpool accents straight away. Off we went through locked and coded doors, corridors and corners. On the way to the transport, I asked one of the policemen for a light. 'Fuck off,' he said. When we got to the cage I had to travel in I asked again for a light. 'Fuck off, beast,' said the copper. The police at Stalybridge had obviously told my escorts that I was guilty as charged. What I could not guess was that this information from Stalybridge would affect the nature of my arrival and treatment at the Bridewell.

Along the journey we collected other prisoners from various police stations. To each and every one, the cop said, 'We have a beast on board, lads,' and I became the target of catcalls and obscenities. I tried to ignore them and I felt rather sad that they were prejudging me on the say-so of those at Stalybridge.

When we arrived the van stopped and I was the first to be unlocked from my cage. I picked up my stuff and tried to step out of the van. My bags were whipped away from me and the cop announced, 'Here's your beast.' I was slammed up against a wall without my feet touching the ground, my hands flattened against it. The pressure was relieved a little and I got a gulp of much-needed air. Then someone grabbed my hands, and another twisted them firmly behind my back. I had to bend forward and I was run into the building by about six cops. As we got inside boots started thudding into my head, body, legs and arms and I was swung round a corner, howling with the pain. Boots continued to crash into me and I almost blacked out. I heard female voices shouting, 'Leave him alone, you bastards!'

A door swung open. I felt concrete smash into my face. Wham. It was the floor. Then a boot was stamped on the back of my neck. I was losing consciousness. One more blow would kill me. The pain was so bad that I heard myself thinking, Please let me die.

Again the boots came raining down. One smashed into my head and then I couldn't see. This is it, I thought, this is death. My coat was ripped off me, followed by the rest of my clothes.

The next thing I knew, I could feel a massive banging inside my head. I slowly began to realise that I was still alive – just. Instinct told me to get up and I tried but fell down again. A female voice said, 'Hey-lar.' I couldn't answer because of the pain. There was a banging on the wall and this woman asking what they'd done to me. I couldn't answer. Still I lay there, expecting them to come and finish off my life.

A while later I found some strength and made a big effort to sit up. I failed but I realised finally that I was alive. My body was covered with cuts and bumps. I felt like it had been split in half, but I had to find some way of getting up – or at least of moving. If I stayed where I was my blood might stop circulating properly and I'd have severe problems. Eventually I made it to my feet, swaying and rocking, but I was determined to stay upright.

A good while later two of those brutes came in. Oh, fuck, I thought, not again. They had a white paper suit which they threw on the floor, and said, 'Sign here.' I tried to hold a pen to sign – I couldn't have cared less what I was signing and to this day I don't know what it was. All I could think then was that these two were going to wade in again. I couldn't grip the pen, which fell to the floor.

One cop said, 'Fucking hell, we didn't hurt you.' I managed to make a mark, not my usual signature, and they left without any more violence.

I got into the paper suit and lay down on an area of raised concrete. I didn't dare move again, I was in such pain. Much later I was called on again and took the opportunity to ask for my cigarettes and some coverings for the night. I received neither. In fact, for a long time I was left with no food, water, coverings or cigarettes and no contact with any member of my family or Les.

Eventually the door was flung open and I was whisked out. Here they go again, I thought. I ended up in front of a cop in a room on the other side of the building. He asked me my religion, my parents' names and address, Les's name and address as well as the rest of my family's addresses. I didn't know why this information was wanted nor did I dare ask.

I was taken away again and put into another cell. At least this one had a wooden bench with a two-inch thick mattress. Later they opened the cell door and threw in my clothes. I grabbed them off the floor, and saw blood on my shirt and trousers and tears in my jacket. Having my own clothes back, though, was heartening and I put them on. I felt human again even though these bastards had done everything possible to prove me otherwise.

It was late at night when the door opened again. A plastic cup was put on the bench at the end of the bed along with a couple of digestive biscuits. The tea was undrinkable – it tasted like urine. I ate the biscuits out of sheer hunger.

The following morning I received another cup of the same tea along with something they called 'breakfast'. It was more like animal feed. I got the drink down me. Some time later I was again opened up and a cop said, 'Do you want a shower?' I thought they must be planning another attack but, what the hell, I thought, they can't hurt me any worse than what they have already.

As I was in desperate need of a wash I took the chance. Much to my surprise I didn't get a hammering in the shower but I kept a watchful eye on the two cops with me anyway. My cuts and bruises stung as the water poured over me, but I came out of the shower refreshed and feeling clean. I was handed a razor, comb and disposable toothbrush and was told to give back the razor after I had finished. I was having a shave when I noticed that only one cop was watching me now. He began to ask me questions about my arrest and how I came to be in custody. He would have known about the allegation against me (or he wouldn't have been there) so it wasn't hard to work out that he was trying to see whether I came out with anything different from what I had said in my interview. I told him a few of the details anyway about how Les and I had begged so many people on Mandy's behalf and how I had saved Mandy's life several times but failed once, with tragic consequences. I told him that because I failed once I was now in custody. He wished me luck.

I was taken back to my cell and locked in again. Later a cop appeared at the cell door to tell me that someone was coming to see me. I didn't ask who, it was enough that someone was coming.

Again the cell door opened. Another cop came in and asked me if I wanted anything from the canteen. I told him that I would like some tobacco, matches and writing paper. He asked if I would like anything else. At this point I knew he must be taking the piss, but I played along and said I'd like some stamps, a pen, biscuits and crisps. He wrote it all down and off he went.

About half an hour later he came back with a small box. He sat down in the cell and said, 'Here you are, son.' Much to my amazement, everything I had asked for was in that little box. I couldn't believe that this change in the cops was going to last long.

I lay down on the bed and began to write a long letter to Les. I poured out my heart but said nothing about the beating. I told her that I loved her, Mandy and Natalie very deeply. Please come and see me straight away, I begged. Little did I know that plans had already been made to bring her. I even managed to get the letter posted.

A good while later the cell door opened again. 'Come on,' I was told. I expected another beating but I followed the cop and was told to sit down behind a plastic partition. On the other side my solicitor appeared. I told him what they had done to me but he had already seen the state of me and was shocked. He told me not to worry, that we would get the best possible medical people available to defend me. I begged him to get me out of this place because I was frightened they'd kill me. I was not allowed long with him and was soon taken back to the cell. This solicitor didn't seem sufficiently interested in my case. I did not think he visited me enough, bearing in mind the charge I faced and he did not keep me as informed of developments as I would have liked. I decided to get hold of my family to ask them to find me a different solicitor.

A little while later a cop came into my cell and asked me to sign for the five pounds the solicitor had left me. He asked if I had made a complaint against the police. He said that they had been told that I had complained of physical abuse. I told him that I hadn't – there was no way I was going to put myself at risk of another beating. Then he said, 'Well, somebody has.' It must have been the solicitor. Soon after this they began to treat me a little differently.

Next day I was told to expect a visitor. I thought it had to be my family and felt better. A few hours later I was taken to the visits area and sat down behind a table and another chair, all enclosed in a large Perspex-fronted screen. Moments later I caught sight of my parents and a third person. I was having severe problems believing my eyes. Blonde hair and gorgeous. It was Les. When she saw me her face lit up. They were all led over and let into the little room. I grabbed Les and we held each other tight and kissed. Then I hugged Mam and Dad. Tears flowed and I sat down with Les on my knee as we couldn't let go of each other. Les and my parents saw straight away that I was badly marked. I showed them the state of my legs and feet – I hadn't worn any socks so that they could see easily without me having to take clothes off. If the cops caught on to what I had in mind it would have caused me severe problems.

I told Les not to say anything to the cops about it as it would make it worse for me.

Les told me that she loved me millions and was a hundred per cent behind me. There's no possible way that I had done anything wrong to Mandy, she said. She told me how proud she was of the way I'd treated Mandy. Then she asked if I'd got the message she'd left earlier in the week. 'What message?' I asked. She said that she had phoned to let me know when Mandy was to be buried so that I could go to the funeral, which had taken place. It had been terrible, she said, not having me beside her. I told her I'd had no message. 'Bastards,' she said.

The cops had failed to tell me. I broke down in uncontrollable sobs. I told Mam and Dad and Les that those cops could beat me as much as they liked but they could never beat guilt into an innocent man.

When I calmed down, we talked about my homecoming and getting back to normal. It was so hard to say goodbye to them all. Les had brought me a bag of stuff, which she left with the police. When I got back to the cell I was handed a carrier bag with clean clothes and other bits and bats. I also found a long, loving letter from Les. I cried my eyes out at the sheer strength of her love for and support of me. Then I got changed into clean clothes and felt something like normal for the first time since my arrest.

The rest of my time at this horrible place was made a little easier by seeing my brother and his wife Gayle of whom I must make a very special mention. She has given me such tremendous support and shown such courage, daring to tread where angels fear. She was also great to Les too. I also saw my sister Janice and her husband Kevin. Janice has been another staunch supporter of my campaign, which will become clear throughout the book.

I received regular letters from Les, full of love, support and comfort. This meant so much to me and I was filled with immense pride at every letter she sent. In return I wrote her mammoth letters, equally full of love for her and the children. Les wrote about her anger at my continued remand; she wanted me home because I had done no wrong. And, after all, if Les could not tell the truth, who could? And here it was in each and every letter, repeated over and over again.

CHAPTER

·················

5

IT WAS AROUND June 1991 that I was shifted out of the Bridewell. You can't imagine my joy at getting out of that place. I didn't mind where they put me after that: nothing would come close to the brutality of the Bridewell. I was taken to Grey Mare Lane police station in Manchester, which was much better for me as I was close to my family – apart from my parents in Wales – and Les. Yet again, though, here was another cop shop that became significant in my case. I was in a cell on my own for most of the time but I saw a lad razored and another beaten while I was there. This, however, was done by prisoners and not the police.

For the first day or so, I was cut off from the rest of the prisoners and the flap on my door was kept closed for those first few days. I saw Les and my family frequently and it was great to see Les on her own. There was a problem though: a plastic partition kept us separate during visits so that we couldn't touch or kiss or hold each other at this time of great need. I thought that was more than cruel. After visits Les would go and sit in the café across the road from the police

45

station where she would sit with a drink and write loving letters to me. Then she would come back and hand the letter in for me.

After a few days, I was called in to see a solicitor and a barrister, my new team. Keith and Gayle had found them. I had to talk to them, too, through the plastic screen. The barrister asked if we could have a room with better facilities, but was refused.

They asked me to go through all the events in Mandy's life again and especially what had happened on 15 April 1991. I gave them everything I could but when it came to 15 April I couldn't control myself. My feelings came out in a flood but I knew I'd have to get used to the pain, because it was clear that I would have to go through this over and over again. I also described the violence meted out to me at the Bridewell, which was still evident in the form of the marks on my body.

The barrister said that he would be representing me at committal proceedings to take place before Dukinfield Magistrates' Court in July.

Mysteriously, Les's letters were less regular than they had been but she visited fairly often. Once she told me that she had just got back from seeing my solicitor. Neville had gone with her. They were told that I was completely innocent. But Les, of course, already knew this.

As the committal date neared Les's letters and visits were few. I couldn't understand what was going on. Gayle and Keith had seen my solicitor about the committal hearing and reported that a strong bail application would be made. My barrister was going to try and get the case thrown out of court.

The committal hearing took place on 23 July 1991. I was taken to Dukinfield Court and put in a cell. Later I saw my barrister, who assured me that he had no doubt that I was innocent, that there was no case to answer and that it was all sheer and utter nonsense. I felt good at this comment because it showed me that he truly believed in me. Then he went off to prepare for the hearing and I was taken back to the cell.

No sooner was I locked in than DCI Walker appeared. He said, 'I believe you had a bad time at the Bridewell,' and smirked at me. He started to ask questions: 'What were you doing for money while you were at home?'

Instead of answering him, though, I asked why I was still in custody. 'I've done nothing,' I told him.

He replied, 'At the end of the day it's down to the doctors.'

'If that's so, why am I still here?' I asked.

He couldn't answer.

He took great pride in telling me that he was opposing bail. 'Why?' I asked, but he gave no answer, just smirked at me again and left. I was locked in to reflect on what he had said.

Later, a young copper came to take me up to the court. He clapped me in a pair of handcuffs and led the way into the dock. The handcuffs dug into my wrists and he kept pulling at them to tighten them even further. My hand went numb as this kid pulled. I was sat down with him next to me – he made sure that he was in a good position to yank on the cuffs occasionally.

I took in the surroundings of the courtroom and saw my family with Les's parents and Les. My barrister was more or less in front of me with Walker, who was talking to some cronies. I mouthed to Les, 'I love you' and she mouthed back, 'I love you too.'

The magistrates arrived and took their seats. No sooner had they sat down than the prosecutor jumped up and began to read out my record for petty offences when I was younger. This was in clear breach of the 'assumption of innocence' but no one tried to stop him. Even more bizarre was that he told the bench I was in breach of a suspended sentence. He went on to say that I had killed Mandy, even though my defence

47

had been given no evidence to support this. I couldn't believe what he was saying and simply shook my head in disbelief. But he still hadn't finished: he told the court that I had shaken and punched Mandy which had resulted in her death, and that these were the findings of Dr Freeman and Dr Garrett. The bench asked to see the two doctors' statements.

Meanwhile, the young policeman was pulling harder on the cuffs. I had had enough of this so I said loudly, 'Are you trying to break my wrists?' Everyone looked round, much to the copper's embarrassment and he stopped playing the idiot.

The magistrates looked at the statements, then said, 'Unless these two statements are signed they will not be admitted in evidence.' That they were unsigned was news to me but Walker took them and went out of the courtroom. A few minutes later he returned with both miraculously signed. He told the court that the doctors were in the building. How very helpful to the police cause, I thought. Maybe the pathologist was performing postmortems on the steps outside while the paediatrician examined a child in the waiting room.

Then they announced that Les must leave as she was a witness in the case. I, too, was a witness in the case and wanted to get out of this absurd pretence of a committal hearing. It was anybody's guess as to what might happen next.

I saw Les standing just outside the glass entrance doors to the court. We kept mouthing 'I love you' to each other. The bench cast funny looks my way. I looked back at them and thought, You can look at me any way you want but you certainly can't take away your own inept handling of this committal. It was they who deserved funny looks, not me.

The committal continued. The prosecutor concluded a final submission to the bench, opposing bail because of the serious risk that I might interfere with 'witnesses'. The seriousness of the offence and my own safety were also to be taken into account. There was nothing to support any of these claims. First, my family and Les's were sitting together in court. Of them, the only witness was Les, whom the bench had seen telling me that she loved me. Yet the prosecutor said that I might 'interfere' with her! It is also of note that both families believed wholeheartedly in my innocence.

As for my own safety, this would be more at risk if I were remanded in custody, as I knew from the beating administered at the Bridewell. I found it incredible that these people could tell a court of law that they were concerned for my safety after they had almost killed me. Worst of all, the court was only too eager to accept whatever the police put forward.

Then it was my barrister's turn to address the bench. He said straight off that not one point raised by the prosecutor was correct, that there was no reason why I should not be granted bail and that, if needed, sureties were in the court. He pointed to both families and said that there was no possibility of any interfering with witnesses. Strangely, he didn't mention the beating. He put forward a strong case, which, in any other court, would have secured bail. However, in the middle of his speech the magistrates got up and walked out! My barrister was momentarily dumbstruck at this but recovered quickly and said, 'Excuse me, I haven't finished yet.' They came back reluctantly to let him finish but I knew then that there was no way they were going to grant bail. They had heard the police version and that was enough for them.

They retired for a very short time, and returned to inform me that I would be remanded in custody for a trial before a crown court and jury. Bastards, I said to myself, and made a thumbs-down sign to Les. While the chief magistrate was still babbling on I tugged on the handcuffs and asked to be taken down to the cells. I had had more than enough of this charade.

Once there, I saw my barrister who couldn't believe what he had just had to put up with. He said he would make a strong application for bail to a judge-in-chambers.

Les and my family also tried to see me but were refused. I did not find out about this until the next day.

I was taken from the court to Platt Lane police station close to Manchester City's football ground, where I met the other inmates with whom I spent a large amount of time up until my trial.

Gayle and Keith were working hard on my behalf, seeing the solicitor and bringing me news of developments. Gayle learned from him that I had a large medical team working on my defence and I began to feel a little more at ease.

One day Les telephoned the station. For once I was allowed to talk to her. She said that the social services had been to see her and told her that if she wrote, visited or contacted me in any way Natalie would be taken into care and that she would not get her back. Shortly after this, her letters dried up. I saw her once, when she turned up half drunk and said that she had come with a lad. I could understand her need to find consolation somewhere.

She looked me straight in the eye and said, 'Kev, did you hurt Mandy?' I asked her how she could ask me such a terrible question. She had been there when I tried to save Mandy's life and we had been at home together during the week before 15 April. I broke down. Then she said, 'They keep hammering away at me that you battered Mandy and killed her.' I asked her who she meant. 'The police and social services,' she said. They wouldn't leave her alone, she said.

It was evident that Les was under tremendous pressure from the police and social services to turn against me. I couldn't believe that anyone would stoop so low at such a time of grief and loss. She tried to comfort me and kissed me, which is when I realised that she was seeing someone else. The kiss felt different somehow from the way she usually kissed me. Our love had vanished into thin air. I had sort of known that when she asked me whether I had hurt Mandy. I made the visit shorter than normal – the pain was too much.

I went back to my cell. I stood at the bed and put my head in my arms, crying. A cop had seen what was going on and did not lock the door but let me be for a while.

Gayle kept up her constant requests for information to the solicitor and her visits to me. Her tireless efforts ensured a steady supply of clean clothes and as much good news as she could find.

Janice, too, was doing all she could. She brought sandwiches, newspapers and cigarettes and made certain I wouldn't go short of anything. Also while I was at Platt Lane I went through some statements with someone from the solicitor's office. He brought the pathologist's and paediatrician's reports and left everything with me to read and make notes on anything I wanted to draw attention to.

I got friendly with a few lads at this station. One was Martin and the other was Paul. In July I was moved from Platt Lane to Bacup, as were they. We ended up sharing a cell. Paul and I went through all the case papers together.

I managed to phone Les's parents from here. Neville answered the phone but when I asked for Les, he said she'd gone to the Lakes with a lad. I said I would call back at the weekend. When I eventually spoke to her I asked her what she was playing at. She cracked daft and asked me what I meant. I told her what her dad had told me a few days ago but, not surprisingly, she denied it. I talked to her a few times after this. She had got a job in a pub working as a part-time barmaid. Once, when I rang her there, someone else answered the phone. They asked who I was and I told them Les's boyfriend. The voice at the other end said, 'Oh, hello, Martin.' I was stunned.

When Les came to the phone, I said, 'Who the fuck's Martin?' She still denied that she was seeing someone else, but I knew the truth. When I saw her some weeks later, at Bacup, she looked stunning. I had to ask her what she was up to. She played dumb again and told me how much she loved me and couldn't wait for me to come home. But in spite of this, I could see she had no real feelings for me any more.

At Bacup I saw a clerk from my solicitor's, who brought a statement that had been taken by Walker from a Paul Weir, who alleged that he had been at Grey Mare Lane police station at the same time as me, and that I had said to him, 'Mandy was screaming so I shook her.' I neither recognised this person's name nor had made any such statement to anyone at Grey Mare Lane police station during the time I spent there. I knew this statement was wrong. I had not shaken or punched Mandy ever. The only wrong I did was in not being able to bring her round on 15 April.

The clerk told me that this was a 'normal' trick played by the police. He explained that they often got someone to make false allegations. He also left some other statements with me and asked me to go through them. The instant I clapped eyes on them I saw that Les had become a prosecution witness. This I could hardly believe. Her statement, though, was very much in my favour as it told nothing but the truth.

I phoned her and asked her what she was playing at now. She told me that she hadn't known she was a prosecution witness until she got a letter telling her and that the police had said to her that it 'doesn't matter' that she's a prosecution witness.

'Look, Les,' I said, 'it matters a lot to a jury.'

She said there was only the truth in the statement, but I knew that her appearing for the prosecution would make us look very distant from each other, which would not help my case in court. But I was wasting my time trying to make her see the damage this could do to me, and for the rest of my time at Bacup Les did not write to me.

Paul and I continued working through the case papers together and constantly made notes and points. It was very helpful for me to have his neutral opinion. He believed that I was innocent of hurting Mandy and was a big support to me, which I valued when Les seemed to have given up on me.

One day a sergeant came to the cell door and told me to pack my things. Not another merry-go-round move, I thought, but instead he told me that I was to be released on bail. I packed at lightning speed, went to the desk where the sergeant was sitting and signed a release form. I phoned Gayle and asked her to come and collect me, then went out of the station, leaving my box of property on the step.

I hadn't known that the bail application to the judge-in-chambers was to be heard that day, so it all came as a complete surprise. I went down to the shops and bought some cigarettes and matches, then phoned my parents to tell them I was out. They were thrilled and said my bedroom was ready and waiting and that we'd see each other later. I was waiting for Gayle at the bottom of the street where the police station was when all of a sudden a voice shouted from behind me. I looked round and a cop gestured that he wanted me. I went back into the police station and was told I was wanted on the phone.

I picked up the receiver. 'This is Sergeant Jones from the North Wales Police at Llandudno. I have to tell you that sureties have not been lodged and you will have to be taken into custody until such time as they are,' and I was taken back into custody.

When Gayle arrived, I told her what had happened. She said not to worry, she would use her own home and Janice's as surety. I asked her to be quick – I didn't want to spend a moment longer than I had to in that place – and she rushed off to get the documents together. Then she and Janice went to Ashton-under-Lyne police station and presented the documents only to be told that they knew nothing about the matter and that Gayle and Janice would have to go to Stalybridge where my papers were, which they did. The same thing happened there.

When I contacted my solicitors the next day, I told them about the bail and the surety problems to discover that they hadn't known that bail had been granted! But someone from the solicitor's must have been at the hearing, otherwise I would not have been granted bail.

I was not released on bail from Bacup, and was not surprised when I heard that the fella in charge of the case had phoned up and said that I was not to be released without his say-so.

While I was at Bacup my solicitor arranged for me to see a psychiatrist. I had no idea why until the appointment when the psychiatrist told me he had to see me to decide whether I was fit to plead at my trial. Some of the things he had me doing were outrageous: he asked me to count backwards from a hundred to zero, subtracting nine each time – I did this with ease – then he asked what the capital of England was. I replied, 'Gary Lineker,' and we both had a laugh. I had to name some European capital cities – here I was in my element, and I think he didn't know I was a European trucker.

He also asked me about Mandy and my relationship with her, Les and Natalie. I told the whole story once again of how badly we had been treated in our pleading for help with Mandy, how her health went downhill before our eyes and how horrified Les's and my family had been at the authorities' lack of interest in Mandy's plight.

I had a few more meetings with the solicitor's clerk while I was at Bacup, which were not very productive. Once he brought the ante- and postmortem photographs of Mandy to show me. I saw immediately that scratches and cuts had appeared on her face in the postmortem photos which weren't there in the ante-mortem ones. I told the clerk but he appeared not to fully appreciate what I was saying.

It wasn't long after this that I was on the move again. This time it was to the dreaded Strangeways prison in Manchester. About five of us were taken there that day, all in the same van, so the journey wasn't too bad as we knew each other. When we arrived, we were locked in a room together. After a bit, we were called to a desk, one at a time, where we were processed and then taken to another room. One lad was called to the desk, then went to another room from which he reappeared with his prison kit of blankets, plastic cup, spoon, knife and fork, towel and soap. Suddenly a group of lads pounded into him and battered him to the floor. When they'd finished with him they came to the room where we were waiting and said, 'No worry, lads.' The rest of us were processed without any incidents. Then we saw a governor. He laid down the law to us all and asked each of us our charge. We were all to be placed in the VP – vulnerable prisoners' – unit, where inmates are housed for their own protection.

When we got there I recognised some of the lads there from other remand places where I had been kept. We were all paired off into twos and I was with a lad called Olbie. We were to share a cell once again. He had been at Bacup with me so I knew at least that I would be in good company. I saw Martin and Micky there too – Micky was the lad who got razored at Grey Mare Lane.

We were to be 'paid' once a week, which would entail us going into the main prison canteen where other prisoners, also unconvicted, bellowed abuse and all sorts of sick names at us. It was hard to accept that people who themselves had not yet been found guilty at trial could behave like this to others in the same situation – they seemed to have found us guilty without trial. In any event I settled down quickly at Strangeways, even though we were locked up for endless hours at a stretch.

I wrote to Les to tell her where I was and that I would like to see her. I also asked her to write to me, but received nothing. Once I managed to phone her at the pub where she was still working. She told me again that she still loved me and couldn't wait to have me home. I asked her why she hadn't replied to my letters. She said that she had.

'When are you coming to see me?' I asked.

'Soon,' she said.

I told her that I needed her support very much.

Much to my surprise, she did visit me one day. I was so pleased to see her and she wouldn't let go of me. She had brought some photos of herself for me to have in my cell. I thought she looked very fat in them and told her so, which embarrassed her, for some reason.

I tried hard to get Les to visit again but she wouldn't, using all the excuses in the world. I even managed to get a probation visit sorted out but she still wouldn't come. Finally I got hold of her one night at the pub.

'Kev,' she said, 'I've got something to tell you. Kev, I'm pregnant.'

I was devastated, but I said I would stand by her. Her 'excuse' for this pregnancy was a joke: she had been to a party, she said, and gone to bed where she had fallen asleep only to wake and find a lad in bed with her.

Les came to see me at the next probation visit I set up, and told the probation officer, Margaret, how good I was with her and the children and that I had never harmed any of them. She held my hand tightly throughout this visit and took pride in telling me that our home had been redecorated for my homecoming and she couldn't wait for me to be there with her. This time she promised she'd write regularly. I felt a bit happier after I'd seen her because I knew at least that Les was in no doubt about my innocence. However, our relationship was dead by this time. I had no more letters, and contact stopped.

It was getting to the end of 1991 when I had a meeting with my junior barrister, Marc, who told me that the medical evidence was good but needed tightening up a little. He told me that no jury in the world could convict me. The only way that I could be found guilty, he said, was if I pleaded guilty.

A few weeks later I had a letter from my solicitors telling

me that no stone had been left unturned and my medical experts were fully briefed for the trial. It ended with a paragraph that gave me some hope. A full and strong bail application would be made at a pre-trial review which had been set for November/December 1991. I might even be home for Christmas.

The review, though, did not go in my favour. Judge Rhys Davies was presiding at Manchester Crown Court. All my family were there in support. Just before the judge made his grand entrance we were all told, 'Please rise,' and 'All be seated' after he'd got to his place. I sat myself down to hear a load of legal jargon read out. I was at a loss to understand what it meant, although one thing was quite clear: 'Kevin John Callan, please stand.' I stood up and the following words boomed across the courtroom: 'Do you plead guilty or not guilty to the charge of murder?' I straightened and replied firmly, 'Not guilty,' and was told to sit down. My barrister asked for certain documents regarding Mandy's medical history to be released to the defence. The judge agreed as they were important to my case, but I never saw them then and, as far as I am aware, they have not even now been made available. If we had been able to see them when we asked to do so, I have no doubt that the evidence presented before the trial court would have been questioned seriously.

My barrister then brought up the subject of bail. He told the judge that I had been granted it in July 1991 but, due to problems regarding the sureties, I was still in custody. The judge said he was very concerned at the length of time I had been in custody but that my barrister should see him in his chambers the next week to resolve the issue. Such was his concern at my prolonged incarceration that he kept me in custody!

However, no further approach was made to the judge for my bail and I was given no reasons for this and had no contact from my solicitor or barrister. I felt like shit at the prospect of spending Christmas in a place like Strangeways. I coped, somehow. In any case, I had to brace myself for the trial, which Judge Davies had set for Wednesday, 15 January 1992. On top of this I had to force myself to forget that Les would be spending Christmas with another man and that I would be apart from all my family, but the hardest part of all was trying to understand why Mandy had had to die.

CHAPTER

·················

6

NINETEEN NINETY-TWO finally came, much to my relief –
I'd had enough of 1991. I was still sharing a cell with Olbie,
who told me I'd woken him during the night crying out for
Mandy.

I was seen by a female doctor at Strangeways, who wanted
to discuss aspects of the case with me. She told me that this
was standard procedure as she had to produce a report on me
for the trial. I told her about everything that had happened
with Mandy and of my close relationship with her, Les and
Natalie. We came to the subject of haemorrhage; the alleged
cause of Mandy's death. What she told me about this subject
is firmly implanted in my brain. Mandy could, she said, have
had a haemorrhage on a number of occasions dating back to
November 1990 – the fall at school. Why, I wondered, was I
in a prison cell if this was true?

Near the trial date I saw a QC, who came across as arrogant. He said that he had met with a pathologist, who had told
him that no other explanation for Mandy's death could be
considered other than that I had hurt her. A fall could not

have caused the alleged haemorrhage that led to her death. He went on to inform me that if I pleaded not guilty I would be found guilty of murder and that he would see the prosecution with regard to them accepting a manslaughter plea. I told him that I could not plead guilty to something I had not done. 'I don't care what you plead,' he said, 'I still get paid. In fact, I would prefer it if you were to plead not guilty as I would earn more money.' I took a lot of interest in the man who had accompanied the QC to this meeting, noting his reactions to what was going on around him.

The QC's attitude badly affected my confidence in his ability to represent me. He advised me who he would and would not be calling to give evidence at the trial, and I got the impression that I had little choice in the decision. Before he left, I repeated that I would not, under any circumstances, plead guilty to something I had not done and nor would I accept a manslaughter charge.

A few days later my solicitor turned up unexpectedly. He knew about the pressure being put on me by the QC. I guessed that the man who had been with the QC had told my solicitor of what had gone on. I said, 'I have done no wrong and will neither plead guilty nor have this QC represent me at the trial.' Both the QCs whom I had originally wanted to represent me were busy on other cases but the solicitor said he would find a good one for me.

The day before my trial, I met Jack Price, the QC who would represent me, with another man and a woman. From listening to Jack it quickly became clear to me that he did not seem to know all the intricacies of my case, but he said that he would stay up all night to familiarise himself with it. I truly felt totally lost and defeated. Jack told me that it was going to be difficult to convince a jury of my innocence – extremely difficult, he added. What I couldn't understand was how it would be difficult to convince anyone that Mandy would be alive if medical action had been taken when asked for.

*

On 15 January 1992, I was put on a coach and taken to Manchester Crown Court for the start of a serious miscarriage of justice. We arrived at the court building to be halted by two automatic electronically operated concertina gates. The gates were opened and we drove in. I was taken off the coach and put in a cell on my own until I was taken to see my defence team, Marc Leon and Jack Price QC along with the woman. They told me they would give it their best shot. But would their best shot see the truth come out? I asked myself. Then I was taken back to the cell to await my call to the court before His Honour Justice Leonard.

While in my cell prior to the trial starting, I had a book to read and my inner thoughts to contend with. Although I had the book open, I had no hope of reading it as my mind was going haywire at the thought of having to face a court of law on such an absurd charge. I felt as though my heartbeat could have been heard from miles away, such was the fear of the unknown. My head was banging away like a steam train, massive poundings inside it to the stage where I was going dizzy.

I thought about the prospect of seeing Les again. Oh, fuck, this made me even worse. I was totally puzzled and confused. 'Don't worry,' I told myself, 'you will be back with her in a few days.' I thought that the trial would be stopped very soon because it should not even begin. 'Will it begin?' I asked my pounding head. 'Am I dreaming this bad dream or am I in a living nightmare?' No answers could be found or heard because there were none.

As I waited for the trial there were hundreds of thoughts going round in my mind: There is no way that this trial can result in anything but my innocence being loudly shown. They will see that it is all so wrong, so fucking wrong. I have done nothing wrong and yet I am having to face this load of bollocks. Justice! This, justice? What justice? If there was any then I would not be here shitting myself, being excited at the prospect of seeing Les again, being with my family again. What if they get it all wrong and send me to prison?

I was more than confused, I was totally gone. I began pacing a million miles in a tiny coffin. I was called to see my legal team. Off I trooped to the so-called interview room. There was the QC, junior counsel and a female representative of the acting solicitors. The QC sat me down and began to explain that it would be difficult, very difficult, to convince the jury to find me not guilty. 'What?' I said. 'How the hell can I be found guilty for something that I did not do. I don't believe this. One minute I am told that no jury in the world could find me guilty, then I am told that it will be very difficult to convince them to find me not guilty.' He said he would give it his best shot. That was practically the end of the interview. I was trooped off back to the cell and locked up again.

The pacing began again. My head hammered even more now. What the shit is going on with this, one big balls-up? I thought. I could not get my head round all this nonsense about being found guilty. I remembered hearing about other cases where innocent people had been wrongly convicted. It was like having a conversation with the invisible man. These feelings of all the negativity surrounding me were making me even more confused and twisted. Jesus, I was so screwed up now. Even my legal team had been so negative, something I didn't expect after hearing their more positive words throughout my remand period.

It hit me like a bulldozer that it was a real possibility that I could be wrongly convicted. At least I had the judge and jury to rely on, didn't I? Regardless of what may or may not happen, I had something inside me stronger than anything in this world: INNOCENCE.

My name was duly bellowed from some unknown place. The door was unlocked and I was taken through underground tunnels, gates, locked doors until I was finally told to stand where I was. I could hear talking from above. All of a sudden I was taken up some stairs. At the top, I almost shit myself at the sight that greeted me. I wanted to turn and run as the sheer enormity of the situation and fear took me over. People with wigs on and people with black silk gowns on. Oh, shit, I thought. I took a glance around my new surroundings. I saw my family and Les's family along with Les and that big fat pregnant belly. I felt a touch of something like a weird normality when I saw Mam and Dad.

I was told to sit down on a bench with rails directly in front of me. My QC and barrister were quick to recognise my fear: they both said hello and told me I'd be OK. Like fuck I will, I thought. They gave me a brief run-down of which witnesses were to be called first. I could feel myself shaking with fear. I turned round and saw Les watching me. 'I love you,' I mouthed. No reply. Fuck it, I thought. I had a word with my family, who were to my left. I saw Les move over to my parents but then my head spun round to locate the owner of the voice which suddenly boomed, 'All rise.' In a corner of the court I saw a man in a black suit standing at a door – it had been him speaking. I stood up, the door opened – and again I could have run and I really did want to. Fucking hellfire, oh no, I thought. This red-robed person walked in with a wig on his head. The gowns and wigs below me bowed to their God. Get me out of here, please. My legs began to go on me. My hands were shaking and I was twitching like a schoolboy in front of the headmaster for the very first time. This was the effect upon me of the arrival into the courtroom of one Mr Justice Leonard. 'All be seated,' the voice boomed.

I was asked to stand and a charge of murder was read to me. I was shaking like a leaf and shifting from one foot to the other. 'How do you plead to the charge?' I was asked. I made no mistake in the quality of my reply. 'NOT GUILTY,' I boomed back. One by one the jury were sworn in and I was asked if I had any objection to any of the twelve people. I didn't so we were under way.

The prosecution QC was Mrs Grindrod. She set out her case against me in tones I felt to be of rage and disgust. She described the witnesses who would be called to give evidence for the Crown and told the jury that although there was no direct evidence of my guilt in this case, a person would give the court details of a confession from my lips. A confession from my lips? I couldn't wait to see this lying bastard who was to tell of a so-called confession. But I had to wait for that. Mrs Grindrod called her first witness.

'Call Miss Lesley Sharon Bridgewood.'

I felt a surge of pain as Les walked the short distance from her seat to the witness box. She was heavily pregnant for all to see. After she had taken the oath, she described our relationship and my relationship with the children. The prosecutor tried to get her to say that I was violent, but Les had none of it and spoke nothing but the truth. She praised my handling of the children and herself. The judge butted in to ask if she would like a seat but she said no, and carried on talking about the minor miracles I had achieved with Mandy. The prosecutor was beginning to understand that she wasn't going to turn against me, so she turned on Les. Les described the events of 15 April 1991 and again praised my efforts to keep Mandy alive.

'Did he not attack your daughter?' asked Mrs Grindrod.

'No, never.'

'Did he hit any of the children?'

'No.'

'Did he hit you?'

'No.'

'Would you say he was a good father figure?'

'Yes, he was a very good father figure.'

'Are you telling me that he never once hit the children?'

'Not even tapped them. His patience was his best feature.'

'And that he never once hit you?'

'Never.'

This was not what Grindrod had wanted to hear as it did not support her unfounded allegations against me of murder.

Now Jack Price cross-examined Les. She described the severe problems Mandy had with mobility. She needed special equipment to have any hope of achieving the everyday nor-malities of life and I had been a tremendous support to her and the children, she said. I showered both children with affection. She again described, more fully this time, how Mandy had gone white, with her eyes rolling, on the swing on 15 April, and how I tried to resuscitate her. Importantly, she remembered the medic telling me to 'carry on, mate, you're doing a good job', while I was trying to get Mandy to breathe. Mysteriously, this comment had not appeared in the medic's statement, nor had his request to his assistant for a suction unit as Mandy's airway was blocked. Les's evidence contained nothing but the truth.

Next to be called was Dr Jeffrey Freeman, consultant pae-diatrician at Tameside General Hospital. Jack Price asked him whether Mandy could have sustained a haemorrhage falling down the stairs. Freeman answered, 'I cannot exclude that. It is a possibility.' Later, under re-examination from Grindrod, Freeman said that a haemorrhage could occur if the head was arrested suddenly in a fall.

Jack Price brought up the question of Mandy being pushed in the swing and her ability to control her neck in this situation. Mandy's condition meant that she had only limited control over her head movements. When this was pointed out to Freeman, he came out with an astonishing comment: 'I must make it clear that Mandy was not my patient prior to her death and, as far as I can make out from a perusal of her notes, which were written by other doctors who had care of her treatment, she had cerebral palsy and spastic diplegia. The meaning of that is that the paralysis, the disability, was more confined to the limbs, inhibiting her walking. As far as I am aware – and you might have to check this with the doctors who were looking after her – her head control was reasonable.'

This told me that Freeman's evidence was based on suppo-sition rather than facts. Supposition which, in my opinion, had the effect of covering up for the doctors who were looking after her, who had failed to respond adequately to our requests for help.

Freeman agreed that Mandy's speech was impaired and that she had little control over mouth and tongue muscles, but he had led the court to believe that Mandy merely had a problem with her walking ability, which, of course, was very far from the truth.

He was then asked by Jack Price whether, after a minor rupturing of blood vessels, further movement of the head could exacerbate the condition, leading to the haemorrhage.

Freeman answered, 'It is theoretically possible.'

Then the prosecutor made an unwitting contribution to Freeman's own confusion about his theory. She said, 'She was treated for various disabilities: attempts being made to strengthen her legs; *correct a squint* . . .' (my italics) which clearly proved to me Freeman's argument to be rather flimsy. As the consultant paediatrician, Freeman should have known full well of the severe problems we had been having with Mandy's health, but appeared to be absent whenever we asked for help. Bearing in mind subsequent events, I have often wondered why he still has a job.

> **Grindrod**: You gave it as your opinion that that double haemorrhage or haematoma in the brain was caused by forcible shaking.
> **Freeman**: Yes.
> **Grindrod**: Is that still your view?
> **Freeman**: It is.

The prosecutor then had Mandy's medical records brought into the case.

Here is another example of my difficulty in coming to terms with the fact that he is still employed.

> **Grindrod**: One of the suggestions which has been made to you in cross-examination is that, arising out of the injury

66

which we know the child sustained on 22 November 1990, there could have been an undetected subdural haemorrhage.

Freeman: Yes.

Grindrod: I think it was also suggested that that could have dispersed and disappeared so that there would be no trace of it.

It is vital that I made exact descriptions of this particular injury. Although she had no symptoms of subdural haemorrhage, Freeman himself had already told us that it was *possible* for Mandy to have had a haemorrhage at this time. The injury had been a 2 cm deep laceration to the crown of the head, a severe injury to anyone but more so to Mandy who had been born with brain damage. Since Mandy's birth she had been under the Tameside Hospital, yet all they had done at that hospital for that injury was to stitch the wound and send her straight back to school! There had been no observations, brain scans, instructions given to Les and me as to how we should care for a head injury – nothing.

Freeman had already admitted that Mandy could have had a haemorrhage in November 1990. Observation, scan, X-ray and tests should have been automatic. They were not. They were not even considered – and I ask myself why, why, why?

We moved on to the next admission to the same hospital in March 1991, when both Mandy and Les went in, Les for her D and C and Mandy for what we were promised would be two days of tests relating to her symptoms following the injury in November 1990. It was established that Mandy was on the ward for 'observations' but Freeman said that the reasons for Mandy's admittance were her crying and a decrease of appetite.

I knew that I was up against it now. I had to accept that the jury would be lost on hearing these complicated medical explanations. I can even remember the judge had to keep interrupting for further explanations because he seemed to find it hard to understand too. Nothing made any difference:

the professionals were for the prosecution and I was on my own. What chance of my success against this?

The next witness to be called was Dr Geoffrey Garrett, the Home Office pathologist. He spoke of his 'thirty years' experience as a pathologist' and the twenty years he had spent with the Home Office. He described the marks he found on Mandy at postmortem: the bruising on both the outside and the inside of much of her body and the blood clot on her brain.

However, if I had thought Freeman's evidence was bad, I was soon shaken back to reality by Garrett.

Grindrod: I think you found the respiratory system was normal?
Garrett: Yes.
Grindrod: The cardiovascular system was normal in size and shape?
Garrett: Yes.
Grindrod: Nothing of note to report there?
Garrett: That is correct.

However, in Garrett's postmortem report, dated 17 April 1991, is a section that reads:

Respiratory System
The trachea and bronchi contained inhaled food. The lungs showed areas of collapse.

Nothing of note to report there? I find it surprising that a pathologist finds lungs partly collapsed with inhaled food in the airways and says that there is nothing to report. In my appeal, it was established that airway obstruction could have been a factor that contributed to the fatal changes which led to Mandy's death, yet Garrett said the respiratory system was normal.

He went on to describe bruising to the stomach and the small intestine, and a small tear to the liver. Again, in his post-mortem, this is noted as:

> The bruising within the abdominal cavity is consistent with a hard blow to the upper abdomen shortly before death.

Grindrod: Did that correspond with any external bruising?
Garrett: Yes. This corresponds to the bruising on the abdomen. Particularly that which is in the middle of the body.

It must be obvious to anyone that, if you are put in a life-or-death situation, inevitably you will do everything to save that life and even more so when it is a child's life. The marks on Mandy's chest and abdomen were a direct result of Les's and my untrained efforts at resuscitation. Our neighbour had also made an attempt, and so did the medics who arrived by ambulance, and others at the hospital.

Grindrod: We know that there were attempts made to resuscitate this child, apparently by in some way putting pressure on the chest. Do the signs of marks on the chest, in your view, appear to or could they be the result of resuscitation?
Garrett: Yes. The marks on the chest are consistent either with knuckles or fingertips and it is possible that they were caused by attempts at resuscitation.
Grindrod: What about the split in the liver?
Garrett: That again I have seen in other children where vigorous attempts at resuscitation have been made.

Why, then, had Garrett made the point in his postmortem report that 'the bruising within the abdominal cavity [had been] consistent with *a hard blow to the abdomen* shortly before death' (my italics)?

Garrett went on to exclude any bump to the head as being a cause of an alleged haemorrhage. He said that in his opinion a fall down the stairs could not be responsible for any alleged haemorrhage: such a fall would have to have been a fall from the top of the stairs with 'violent shaking as the child landed'. He went on to say that he would have expected a fracture of the skull to have occurred if Mandy had died from a haemorrhage as a result of a fall of this kind.

He also dismissed the fall from the slide as being the cause of Mandy's haemorrhage.

Grindrod: If the child, in the course of the afternoon, fell from that slide on to the grass which we see in Exhibit one – first of all, let us consider fell from the steps, the child herself being three feet tall, on to the grass, and was found lying on her side on the grass, could that have caused, in your view, those injuries to the brain?
Garrett: I think it most unlikely.
Grindrod: Why do you say that?
Garrett: The height, I think, is insufficient to have caused such shaking of the brain. I cannot envisage this type of haemorrhage occurring without shaking.

Mandy was three feet tall, the slide was three feet tall. In my arithmetic that makes a total falling height of a possible six feet. Garrett said that this is 'unlikely to cause a haemorrhage'. I say that Garrett is very wrong indeed, considering the height, and the fact that Mandy had brain injury from birth and a history of falls. Garrett's unfounded explanation of the cause of Mandy's death was shaking. He was extremely dogmatic about this, something for which he was criticised at the appeal.

In the lunch break I felt that I could detect flaws in the evidence of the medical experts. Back in that same tiny coffin again, I believed that there were some positive things happening. I had heard different hypotheses being put forward by the medical experts; I had heard hesitancy in the explanations of the pathologist and paediatrician and Garrett had contradicted some of Freeman's evidence. If I could see that then the judge and jury could clearly see it too, couldn't they? I thought. I was determined not to get into the state I was in earlier and I managed to keep a bit of sanity as I thought about the medical evidence that had been given.

When it was time to go back into the courtroom I began to feel the nerves getting at me again. However, I had got through the morning so I could get through the afternoon, surely. I was trying to keep my thoughts positive.

After lunch, in Garrett's cross-examination, Jack Price wanted to know if, having suffered one injury (the fall down-stairs), Mandy's condition could be exacerbated by a second injury. Garrett did not think this was likely and said that the two blows to the head should be treated as separate incidents.

> **Price**: But if, for instance, the person has sustained one blow or one disturbance to the blood vessels, might he be more prone or vulnerable if he sustained another blow shortly afterwards?
>
> **Garrett**: That does not appear to be the case, no.
>
> **Price**: How do you mean – in this particular case?
>
> **Garrett**: No, in cases in general.
>
> **Price**: So if you have already sustained one blow it does not mean to say that if you then go and fall again you might sustain another?
>
> **Garrett**: No. It is a completely separate incident.

Garrett was speaking generally, but he still maintained that the two falls did not contribute to Mandy's death. He insisted that she died because she was shaken.

We returned to the fall from the slide on 15 April.

> **Garrett**: I think an awful lot of children fall off slides of this type without sustaining head injuries.

Price: That may be so. A lot of children have total control of their bodies, have they not?
Garrett: Yes.
Price: This little girl could hardly use her left arm?
Garrett: I am not aware . . .
Price: Did you not know that?
Garrett: I knew that there was a cerebral disability; I did not know the extent.

If he did not know the extent of Mandy's disability, how then had he been able to exclude possible causes of the alleged haemorrhage and the injury? Why was Garrett not aware of these facts?

Jack Price's point was that most children falling off slides could put out both hands and tense their muscles. Mandy could not do this so her fall would have been heavier. Garrett said that he would have expected Mandy's skull to have been fractured if she had fallen from her slide.

Price: It is possible that it might not be fractured?
Garrett: It is possible.
Price: Falling head first, for instance, off that slide on to a grass surface could cause a subdural haemorrhage?
Garrett: I would think it is unlikely.
Price: But you could not exclude it?
Garrett: No.

Other witnesses in the trial also played their part in my conviction. Steven Hague, my ex-brother-in-law, alleged that I had thrown Mandy across the living room. What he had not allowed for was that records prove that Mandy was in hospital with Les at the time he said I had done this.

Gillian Hague, my ex-sister-in-law, told the court that she thought I was cruel to Mandy because I made Mandy do things which were difficult for her. When it was pointed out to Gillian that Mandy's physiotherapist had shown me how to teach Mandy to do things for herself, such as standing up to keep her muscles in tone, exercising her lips by reading words on cards, using her left hand, she told the court, 'I didn't know.'

I finally got to hear the witness who had details of a confession from my lips. All of a sudden there was a lad in the witness box.

'Who is that?' I asked Marc Leon.

'Paul Weir,' he replied.

'Who?' I said. 'I do not remember ever having seen him in my life.'

Paul Weir stated in his evidence that when I was at Grey Mare Lane police station on remand I had told him that Mandy was 'screaming so I shook her'. He was asked why he hadn't reported this at the time and he answered that he had told someone at another police station several months after the alleged event . . .

Our next-door neighbour, Margaret, had also made a statement, which was read out to the court. She said, 'I heard nothing untoward from Number 33 all day.' So, it seems that only Weir and Walker knew of any scream.

Dr McClure, Mandy's own GP, said that she had been told of no symptoms relating to Mandy's deterioration in health.

The judge asked the jury to leave the court and asked the doctor the question again. 'What symptoms were told to you, Doctor?'

'None,' she replied.

The judge asked the usher for the doctor's notes. He asked her if they were her notes about Mandy.

'Yes,' she replied.

'Is this your writing?' he asked.

'Yes,' she replied.

'Well, Doctor,' he said, 'not only are all the symptoms mentioned in your notes but there is also information concerning contact being made with the hospital and the hospital returning information regarding those same symptoms.'

She replied that it was not contained in the case records – from which the judge had just read it out to her.

The two policemen who had been at the hospital had produced their version of what I had told them. It was ten lines long but I had spent a long time with them and had given them graphic descriptions of all the events from Mandy's fall at school in November 1990 up to 15 April 1991. It would have been impossible to get all that on only ten lines and, sure enough, the descriptions had all gone. All their version contained were the events in the bathroom when I was trying to keep Mandy alive.

Finally, it was my turn to go into the witness box. I was so scared.

The prosecutor, a sullen looking female, soon got stuck into me. She made me look a right idiot. She began with my relationship with Les.

'You didn't move in with her straight away, did you?'

'Yes,' I replied, 'more or less.'

'You did,' she remarked, surprised.

'Yes,' I again replied.

'Oh,' came her reaction.

Already she had made me feel ill-at-ease and I felt that she was trying to make the jury disapprove of me.

I was handed a photograph of our back garden which was overlooked by the house opposite us. There was a fence between our gardens which stood about five feet high.

'You said that you had a clear view of the back garden,' she smirked.

'Yes, quite clear,' I answered.

'Members of the jury, it is not a clear view to me.' Turning to me, she said, 'How could you see over the fence?'

'I couldn't,' I replied.

'So you could not see the back garden then,' she triumphed.

'Oh yes, quite easily,' I replied.

'You could not. Is that not your home in the photograph?'

'No, it is not.'

'Which is your home then?'

I told her that the photo was taken from *inside* our back garden, looking towards the house opposite. She changed the subject pretty quickly!

I was handed a small oblong photo album and told to open it.

Bang! I was faced with a photo of Mandy, taken after the postmortem. My legs went as I felt all queasy. I felt tears rolling down my cheeks as they are now when I think of what I was made to do in the courtroom. She made me go through more photos, horrible photos, not the photos I had been used to seeing of Mandy.

'Not very nice, are they?' she asked.

I could do nothing more than simply stare at her.

'Paul Weir,' she barked, 'is the person to whom you confessed at Grey Mare Lane police station. Sometime in April of 1991 you told him that Mandy was screaming so you shook her.'

'I have never seen Paul Weir in my life. What I am telling you is the truth,' I replied.

Hurt though I was by having to look through those photos, I made damned sure that everyone in the courtroom heard the truth. The problem was, though, that the jury believed what the medical experts had told them and Grindrod emphasised this.

'The medical evidence in this case is from a pathologist and a paediatrician. Both have vast experience in dealing with cases and children like this. They both say, and we can't get away from this fact, that something occurred on 15 April 1991 which resulted in the death of this little girl. This was a day that you had sole charge of this little girl.'

'Yes, I had sole charge of her.'

'There was no one else there, was there?'

'No. I was the only person at home for most of the day.'

'So nobody else could have harmed this little girl, could they?' she triumphantly announced.

'Nobody had harmed this little girl,' I replied.

'Oh!' she gestured, surprised. 'You stand there and expect us to believe you? The doctors say that you caused the death of this little girl and that you shook her violently.'

'I did not.'

'That is what they say,' she announced.

'As far as I'm concerned I did nothing wrong on that day. The only wrong I did was that I could not bring her out of an unconscious state,' I declared loudly and truthfully.

Feelings of failure overcame me then, just as they do now. I personally feel that if I had been trained in first aid then I would have stood a better chance of doing something to help Mandy, even though the medical evidence now available says that I could have done nothing. As I told the court, I had done nothing wrong, I had tried to save Mandy's life. To fail in that was bad enough but to face a murder charge was even worse.

The time arrived for the judge to sum up to the jury. He said that Les's evidence had been mainly in my favour and warned the jury to be wary of her evidence. Of Freeman and Garrett, he said to the jury: 'You will take great notice of those two important doctors.' He rubbished anything that supported me because he told the jury that the 'professional doctors' were adamant that shaking had been the cause of Mandy's death. It had not been accidental, he said. It had been deliberate and violent.

Through these outrageous claims, I remained certain that there was no way I could be convicted, because it was not true that Mandy had been shaken or harmed in any way and the judge himself directed the jury to disregard marks on Mandy's body as due to either resuscitation or accidental injury. But he more than made up for that remark by hammering home the version of events given by 'Dr Freeman who, of course, is a consultant paediatrician, an expert in children, and Dr Garrett, the forensic pathologist who has been doing that sort of work for twenty years'. What the judge did not tell the jury was that Garrett and Freeman had no expertise in Mandy, head injury, neurology, neurosurgery, neuropathy or Mandy's health status leading up to her death, all of which have since proved more than relevant.

So, there we were on Monday, 20 January 1992, at Manchester Crown Court. The jury heard the judge's summing up and retired. I was taken down to the cells. After an hour I was told that a verdict had been reached. We went back through all the corridors until we reached the stairs leading to the dock. A call came for us to enter. I was shaking like a leaf as I was asked to stand while the jury poured in with their verdict. My whole life was now in their hands. What would they come up with? I looked at every one of them to try to detect their expressions. I detected nothing. My legs were shaking; my hands were fiddling about behind my back as I stepped from one uncontrollable foot to the other. I was telling myself to expect the worst. Why were they taking so long?

After what seemed like hours, the clerk of the jury stood directly in front of the jury box. 'Will the foreman please stand?' he asked. 'Will you answer my first question yes or no. Have you reached a verdict on which you are all agreed?'

'Yes,' the foreman replied.

'On count one of this indictment do you find the defendant, Kevin John Callan, guilty or not guilty?'

'Guilty.'

I began to sway and collapsed on the bench, became oblivious of everything for several moments. I came to as the judge was telling me to stand.

'You are not the man you presented yourself to be. Unfortunately, there is only one sentence I can pass and that is one of life imprisonment,' he said.

Fuck, fuck, fuck and fuck again, I thought, this is all so very wrong.

The judge asked Jack Price whether there was anything he would like to add in mitigation. He replied, 'I can only add that it was something done on the spur of the moment.'

What the fucking hell did he say that for? Even he was adding strength to the case against me. It showed me just how alone I had been all the time. I had made it clear to Jack Price that I was innocent, yet here he was, more or less agreeing with the case against me.

I managed a glance at my family, who looked as dumb-struck as I was. Then a hand grabbed my arm and I was led away to begin my life sentence. As I left, I caught Les mouthing, 'Bastard, bastard,' at me.

CHAPTER

·················

7

I WAS IN total shock. My mouth was as dry as sand and I couldn't speak. We got to a room within the cell area and I was asked some questions. I couldn't answer. The officer there made me a cup of tea, which helped a little. I croaked, 'What the fuck happened there?' Then I was put into a cell.

A while later I was told that my barrister wanted to see me. He assured me that an appeal would be lodged immediately. Then I was allowed a few minutes with Mam, Dad, Janice, Gayle and Lynn. They were stunned and crying, not able to believe what they had just heard. Then it was back to the cells and I was told I'd be going to the City Detention Centre.

When I got there I could hear radios blaring away, all tuned to the same station. The news was on: 'A man accused of killing his girlfriend's child has been convicted of murder today. Kevin John Callan, thirty-three, a lorry driver, was today convicted of shaking three-year-old cerebral palsy sufferer Mandy Allman to death at their Gee Cross home . . .' Word soon got out that I was that man.

Gayle came to see me later on. As my name was called to go up to the visitors' area, threats came from all sides to kill me or cut me up. But seeing Gayle was just what I needed. We both cried at the sheer horror of the day's events and agreed that, somehow, we would get the truth out. When Gayle left, I had to endure more threats on the way back to my cell.

The following morning I saw a prison screw who told me I would be going to Wakefield Prison.

Later that day I was taken to Trafford police station on the way to Wakefield with some others. The main topic of conversation in the van was the bastard who shook the poor little kid to death. When we got to Trafford I was put in a cell with another lad but it didn't take long for word to spread that I was the child-killer they'd all been talking about in the van so I was moved to isolation on the female side of the police station. A newspaper page was pushed under the door by the lad who brought tea round. The headline was about me and my conviction. Les had added her bit too, saying that if she could get her hands on me she'd kill me. What was going on? Les had been with me, trying to keep Mandy alive, yet here she was wanting to kill me.

Later that night I saw Keith and Gayle again. They had seen Marc Leon and he had told them that an appeal could be lodged straight away which was good news to me. Maybe the truth would come out. They brought me some cigarettes and other bits to help me through. When they'd gone and I was back in my cell, a lad came to the door to tell me that when I got to Wakefield I'd get well sorted out there with a good hiding.

I arrived there several days later after a stop at Runcorn police station, where I saw my parents. They were very supportive and knew that a very big mistake had been responsible for me being in this nightmare. I travelled up the M62 with two screws. I asked them what Wakefield was like and they told me it was OK. When we arrived at the prison, the massive gates opened as if by magic. I was taken out of the van and into the reception area. Two lads behind a counter told me that I would now have to wear prison-issue clothing. I felt a prat because it was all far too big for me.

One asked if I played football. 'Yes,' I said, 'I play in goal.' His eyes lit up and I ended up on D wing – where I later discovered they needed a goalkeeper – in a single cell.

No sooner had I arrived on the wing than a female probation officer turned up to tell me that social services wanted to see me. They arrived on the following Monday and asked if I would go to court for wardship proceedings relating to Natalie and testify that Les was an unfit mother, and had been responsible for Mandy's death. I couldn't believe what I was hearing. There was no reason why Natalie should have been taken away from Les in the first place and no way that I would say any of what they wanted me to say. I thought these people must be setting up some cover-up and kept well away from them.

When I went back to my cell, I wrote a long letter to the trial judge, detailing facts he had not been aware of during the trial. The following morning I was called to the wing office and told that I could only put four sides of paper in any one letter and could send only six letters per week. Welcome to hell, I thought. I had to apply for extra sheets to be placed in my letters. My letter to the judge was finally dispatched in four separate envelopes. He must have thought that I'd gone completely mad. However, much to my surprise, he replied, saying that he had submitted case papers to my solicitors for an appeal.

My next letter was to the Queen. I thought it only right and proper that she should be made aware of the breakdown in our justice system. I was so green that I wrote to several people I thought would take some interest in this miscarriage of justice and used up my week's allowance very quickly. It was immediately evident that I was going to have to obey the rules in this prison and – more importantly – that there would be no help here in contesting my wrongful conviction.

The library was run on a rota system, one wing having a library evening each week. When it was my wing's turn, I asked the librarian what medical books were available, specifically on head injury in children. She suggested several alternatives but the one that took my attention was *Head Injury: The Facts* by Philip Wrightson, Dorothy Gronwall and Philip Waddell. I asked if I could order it and she told me I could but that I would have to get permission from the senior medical officer first. He saw nothing wrong with this and granted permission but I thought it was a bit much that I should have to get permission to borrow a book from the library. It proved, however, more than worth the hassle.

I read that book over and over again. Each time I read it I could see exactly how Les's and my description of the events leading to Mandy's death was undeniably true, and that the evidence given by Garrett and Freeman had been a load of nonsense. My only problem was that the authors of the book were in New Zealand. I wrote to them, anyway, on 1 June 1992. I didn't think that they would be able to help because of the great distance between us.

The prison were generally unhelpful with my attempts at proving my innocence. They agreed to call my solicitors to ask them to come to see me about an appeal – but this was the only positive thing they did. What I did not know was that an appeal had to be lodged within 28 days of the trial, and my solicitors were not as helpful as I would have liked them to be. Also the limit of six letters per week was causing me havoc. I was trying to contact many people within the legal and medical worlds, and I asked for some leeway in this ruling but this fell on deaf ears. I did manage to contact various groups and television programmes who might be interested in my case and my parents and family were doing all they could in that direction too.

One day, I saw an interview in one of our local newspapers with Campbell Malone, the solicitor who freed Stefan Kiszko.

(Kiszko was accused of the murder of Lesley Molseed and spent sixteen years in prison as an innocent man.) Right at the end, Mr Malone made a small but vital comment. He asked, 'How many more Stefan Kiszkos are there in prison?' That was enough for me and I wrote off to ask him to take on my case. It was the beginning of a close relationship – albeit one that had its ups and downs.

In prison, I found it increasingly hard to accept so many petty restrictions while I was trying to prove my innocence but, no matter who I asked, I was still not allowed any more outgoing mail. Finally, I contacted my MP to ask him to intervene on two counts: first on the letters quota and second if he would become involved in my attempt to establish my innocence. He succeeded with the mail but felt he could not become personally involved in my case.

I also wrote to Michael Mansfield, the well-known barrister, to ask him to represent me. He had been too busy to take on my case at the trial, but now he agreed, which gave me a great lift. Then I had a letter from Philip Wrightson, one of the authors of *Head Injury: The Facts*, expressing concern at what I had told him and asking for more information on the case. Wow! This was a major break. I got some bits together and sent them off to him.

By now Campbell Malone was established as my solicitor. He had received the case papers from my old solicitors, Middleweek, and had gone through them. He reckoned it would be difficult to overturn the conviction without an alternative explanation for Mandy's death. I told him of the many medical people I was in contact with. Philip Wrightson had written to me again and had made some comments which have stayed with me to this day. He said: 'The great sadness in what you have told me is that your doubts and fears do not seem to have been recognised and dealt with.' These words were consistent with the events as I described them at my trial and in my statements to the police. From then on, I became deeply involved in books on pathology, brain surgery, neuropathy and cerebral palsy. I had to put up a tremendous battle to justify having these books, but I won. It had become clear to the prison that I was doing my utmost to prove my innocence.

Philip's next letter expressed deep concern at the medical evidence given at my trial and he made a significant offer: 'It has occurred to me that you may like me to get in touch with the lawyers representing you to see whether there were any technical points regarding the head injury that I could comment on.' I sent him Campbell's address and told Campbell that he would be in touch.

Throughout the correspondence between Philip and Campbell, Philip kept me informed about what was going on. The first contact between them was a fax from Philip to Campbell, in which he said he was prepared to look into the case and asked for all medical documentation to be sent to him. Campbell sent him the transcript of Garrett's evidence and his postmortem report, and Freeman's hospital notes of 15 April 1991.

On 6 August 1992 Philip wrote to Campbell: he was, he said, prepared to accept that experienced professional people often misinterpret the relation between their findings and the clinical events and for this reason he thought it worthwhile to look into my case. He also said that he would not expect a fee. It was hard to believe that generosity like Philip's existed, after all I'd endured at the trial. It meant a lot to me that Philip used the word 'we' in his letters when talking about the action that needed to be taken: he included himself as part of a team. And I also got the impression that he had seen through most of the evidence used to convict me at trial.

Around this time, a man turned up from my home area saying that he was now my probation officer. He had taken it upon himself to talk to a nurse about my case, who had expressed extreme doubt about the evidence that had convicted me, as she said a haemorrhage can be caused in many ways. I asked the probation officer to bring her forward but he said that he could not. It was the beginning and end of any relationship between us as I was not going to allow any negative people to jump on my bandwagon.

I received good responses from the Liberty and Conviction campaign groups and I saw a superintendent from the GMP police and told him of the flaws in my case. He listened while I told him about Garrett and Freeman's evidence, then he stunned me by asking, 'Did you kill that child?' I walked out in tears. At least I saw why he had come: he wanted me to confess to a crime that had never been committed.

Now that the prison authorities had to allow me extra mail, it seemed to me that they were getting at me in other ways. Curtains brought by my parents were not allowed in my cell: they were 'too long'. When the curtains came back they were 'too wide'. Gayle brought me a Manchester United bedspread but that was sent back too because, they said, I couldn't have anything with a motif on it! It was clear to me that the people who run these places will deny whatever they can to inmates out of spite and pettiness.

A personal officer was assigned to me. I outlined the case to him and all my problems but his one comment was, 'I cannot get involved.' I found this impossible to accept at a time when miscarriages of justice are of immense concern to one and all. To me, my personal officer's comment showed that the prison system deliberately chooses to ignore innocent men. At the same time, it teaches you how to hate and how to be a criminal if you so choose, while making you bitter, especially if you are innocent, for the experience of a living hell.

I managed to track down the QC who had represented one of those accused of murder in the Strangeways riot trial at which Garrett had given evidence, and wrote to him asking for a transcript of what Garrett had said. When he replied he gave me the address of the medical expert used by the defence but not Garrett's evidence because, he said, one case could not be compared with another.

The expert, Dr Dossett, was based in Leeds, so close to

Wakefield prison. I wrote to him, with as much detail of my case as I could give. His reply told me how unlikely it was that shaking could have been the cause of Mandy's death. This was such important information that I phoned him. He told me that Garrett talks out of his neck and recommended that I approach an expert in Sheffield, Professor Michael Green, with whom he had worked on a similar case in which, between them, they had proved that shock waves had been responsible for a similar injury and not shaking. I passed all this information to Campbell so that he could take it up professionally. Meanwhile I carried on sending letters all over the world to brain surgeons, pathologists and specialists in the field of cerebral palsy and head injury in children. The replies that came in gave me tremendous strength, especially when I saw that every expert reply was along the same lines, that shaking was a very doubtful cause of Mandy's brain injury.

The prison system still put many obstacles in my way. I was refused almost every item that arrived for me – cassettes, typing paper, typing ribbons, Tipp-Ex, anything I needed to help me prove my innocence or that might have made my life in prison a bit more bearable.

I got a surprise visit from Les in November 1992. Her father had been over a few months before, expressing his support. I told her about the evidence that I had amassed and showed her some of the letters I had received. It seemed fairly clear that she was behind me all the way. I couldn't work out, though, why she kept ignoring my letters to her or how she could let someone else find out how her own child had died. If I had been the parent I would have walked to the end of the earth to find out for myself. I thought that if I could make progress from inside a hell-hole like Wakefield, there was no reason why she couldn't do something from outside.

I wrote to the appeal court to try and get some of the

transcripts from my trial. They told me to write to the crown court, who told me to write to the magistrates' court, who told me to write to the appeal court, who told me to get in touch with my solicitors! Was this the way in which the legal system normally operated, I wondered. I wrote back to the appeal court, and they sent me the address of the transcript writers. I asked them for a quote to produce a copy of Freeman's evidence. Four hundred and fifty pounds was the answer. Were they joking? I eventually got the transcript through Campbell, but it turned out that they had wanted all that money for *eight typed pages*. Is it any wonder that so many appeals are abandoned? Fortunately Campbell had managed to secure some funding for me via legal aid but he also put in a vast amount of money out of his own pocket.

At the end of 1992 I received another letter from Philip. He gave me the exact location of Mandy's brain injury and voiced strong opinions on the quality of the evidence he had seen so far that had been responsible for an innocent man being in prison. He told me that Campbell had said all the rest of the medical evidence would be with him soon.

In January 1993 I saw one of the reporters who covered my trial. David Bamber worked for my local newspaper, the *Advertiser*. I told him some of the facts about my case that had since come to light and showed him some of Philip's letters. He was amazed at the inconsistencies in the evidence responsible for my conviction and was visibly shocked at the lengths to which I had gone in my attempt to clear myself. It wasn't long before headlines appeared on the paper's front page, which resulted in several letters to the paper's office in support for me. I also saw Andrew Green of Conviction, the company from Sheffield. He is an unsung hero who has been staunchly active in getting to the bottom of cases like mine and he gave my case a good write-up in Conviction's newsletter. His enthusiasm is refreshing to anyone who has reason to seek him out and he was a good friend to me.

By now I had seen Campbell several times and as the medical evidence we were acquiring was so strongly in my favour it was essential that it should be kept strictly confidential between the medical experts involved, Campbell and myself. We claimed the right to a prison ruling known as SO5B 32(3), which states that the prison may not open mail between client and solicitor unless they have reason to suspect that the contents are not relevant to the client's case. The prison authorities continued to open my legal mail until I had no choice but to refuse mail from my solicitor, which meant I could contact him only by phone and word of mouth.

On 17 February I received another report from Philip Wrightson, which came down heavily against Garrett and Freeman: Garrett's technique left much to be desired; he made no accurate assessment of the brain; he made no microscopic examination; his entire postmortem examination must be regarded as seriously flawed. Philip continued that most neurosurgeons know of instances in which a fall from a children's slide had resulted in significant brain injury even though a skull fracture had not necessarily been present. Pre-existing brain abnormalities make injury more likely in cases associated with cerebral palsy. Philip said that shaking may cause brain injury in infants, but there is some doubt even then, and such incidents are rarely reported over the age of a year. He also remarked that Garrett had made little of the presence of food in Mandy's air passages and lungs, something that was likely to have been a major factor in the rapid development of cerebral oedema. He added, 'It also confirms the account given by Mr Callan of Mandy's rapid deterioration after she began to vomit.' Here was the evidence I needed to justify my release.

In March, I was suddenly summoned by the wing governor. In his office I found two governors and a screw. 'Sit down,' the governor said. The screw was sitting at the table with a piece of paper. He kept pawing at it as if it was something he couldn't keep hold of. The governor lectured me on miscarriages of justice, and rattled off all the notorious cases of recent times for my benefit. He asked me how things were progressing with my case but my shield went up straight away. I wasn't going to tell the bastards how my case stood.

The screw handed me the piece of paper. It had arrived, he said, from the Home Office. When I read it, I discovered that my case was to be reviewed with the Home Secretary. There were doubts as to the safety of the conviction. I went back to my cell with a big beam spread across my face.

The following day I received a letter from Philip Wrightson informing me that he would be sending Campbell a full and detailed report on all the evidence from my case but in the meantime he set out his main areas of comment, with comments from his two colleagues. My stomach was churning as I read:

Two injuries close together may cause cerebral oedema with an increase in intracranial pressure. This may have been contributed to by mild injuries in the preceding weeks. The pressure caused vomiting; with the inhalation of vomit this resulted in a further catastrophic increase of pressure with irreversible brain damage. The abdominal injuries were consistent with resuscitation.

I have discussed the findings with a neuropathologist and an experienced forensic pathologist. Their feeling is that the statements made at trial leave a lot to be desired.

I sat there and wept buckets. Here in front of me was exactly what I had told the police and the court at my trial. I had not been believed at either stage.

As well as Philip Wrightson, I also contacted other experts. The Royal College of Pathologists were sent copies of Garrett's evidence and his postmortem report. They wrote back to inform me that there were areas well worthy of challenge, which supported what Philip had said.

On 18 March I received a copy of Philip's full report from Campbell. It was very long and it took me two to three days to understand it fully but it concluded that Mandy had not died of an injury caused by shaking, that she had not been subjected to physical abuse, and that the evidence given at the trial was unjustifiable. Before my experience, I could never have believed that so much that was wrong in a case could be allowed to convict an innocent man and especially the evidence of experts such as Garrett and Freeman.

I also tried to make some headway on Paul Weir's evidence. He had said that I had shouted out of my cell, 'Mandy was screaming so I shook her,' which was an absurd lie. I asked Greater Manchester Police for Weir's custody record while he was at Grey Mare Lane police station. If his allegation was to be believed then it should have been mentioned in that. But the police would not let me see the record. Like a fool, I told them why I wanted to see it. If I'd known then what I know now, I wouldn't even have asked for the records.

In May Campbell approached another expert of high standing and repute: Helen Whitwell, a consultant neuropathologist and a forensic pathologist who had been pitted against Garrett on several occasions. Much to my delight, I learned that she had never lost a case to him. I waited anxiously for her verdict.

Meanwhile, I had some more medical transcripts which had to be supplied urgently to Philip Wrightson: his evidence was about to be submitted to the Court of Appeal. I saw the legal aid officer, who agreed that I could pay to fax them from the prison to Philip. When he asked the governor, though, he was told that the fax machine was not for everyday use. He argued that it was an urgent legal matter but it made no difference. The case papers had to be submitted to the court without my medical team being able to amend their evidence.

Shortly after this, I sent a visiting order out to Dave

Bamber, the *Advertiser* reporter. However, I was called to the prison office and informed that I would not be allowed to send him either the letter or the VO. Neither was I to see Dave again. Much to Dave's credit, he complained to the Home Office but got no sense from them so he headed the front page of the paper with: 'Our Man Banned From Prison Visits'.

I had a letter from Charles Hunter, the producer of the TV programme *Rough Justice*, who asked to come to see me. I sent him a VO and he came to see me in a private room. No sooner had we sat down than a screw appeared with a piece of paper that said *Rough Justice* would not be allowed to use any material gleaned from our meeting. How the fucking hell can a TV programme be broadcast without the vital information? I couldn't believe the bastards at Wakefield were doing this to me. Charles had to sign the paper, much to my annoyance, but he and a team went to my local area and interviewed several people, including Les and her family, Campbell Malone and my sister Janice. The team were impressed at the level of support for me and I wondered how their next move would show itself.

It was around this time that my sister Janice decided to set up a campaign group in my name. It was called, appropriately, Innocent and held its first meet at Manchester Town Hall on 3 November 1993. In attendance were Michael Mansfield QC, Paddy Hill, one of the so-called Birmingham Six, Campbell Malone and several top lawyers. TV, radio and press were there and the place was packed. The *Manchester Evening News* sent me a cutting with a photo of my sister wearing her T-shirt on which was inscribed: 'Kevin Callan – INNOCENT'.

I saw Campbell that day and he told me that Helen Whitwell was with us a hundred per cent. Helen had concluded that Mandy did not die from being shaken, and that Garrett's evidence had been seriously flawed. I now realised, with the weight of all this medical opinion behind me, how flawed Garrett and Freeman's evidence was.

I was still allowed to see my own two children, Angela and Scott, whom I love with all my heart. When they saw me walk through the door to the visiting room, they would whoop with delight and run at me like mad and I'd burst into tears at the sheer joy of having them there. They too were having a hard time, being teased at school by other kids who had seen the write-ups in the paper. They had been taken into care, because their mother had become heavily involved in drugs.

However, before long, Tameside Social Services told me that I could no longer contact the children and the visits were stopped, even though Campbell had been informed that a visit was being arranged. I have no doubt that Tameside Social Services did this to try to justify what they had already done to me with their unfounded allegations about Mandy. It seems to me that these people have learned no lessons from the well-publicised Orkney and Rochdale child abuse cases; they deny people their children with no evidence to support their actions. My family weren't allowed to see Angela and Scott either.

The end of 1993 left me determined to work with renewed vigour for my conviction to be overturned in 1994 and my first diary entry in the New Year read: 'Freedom and truth'.

I came across a lovely woman, Sue May, from a neighbouring town to my own, whom I'd read about in the Conviction newsletter. She, too, had cause to contest her conviction. It turned out that one Dr Geoffrey Garrett had played a part in her case too, another to be added to the list of miscarriages of justice. Hopefully, the stuff on Garrett that I sent her will help her appeal.

On 25 January Les and her father visited me. I showed Les a substantial amount of the medical evidence which my team and I had amassed. I watched her closely as she read through it. I saw horror and astonishment as the cause of her daughter's death began to hit her. I will never erase the memory of her pain when she saw just how successfully she had been brainwashed into accepting the misleading evidence presented against me at the trial.

When it came time for Les and Neville to leave I asked Les to promise me that she would keep in touch. If she let me down, I said, I would not show her the final medical reports. She promised.

On 31 January Helen Whitwell's final report arrived. She had been allowed access to every conceivable item of relevance and had seen statements, medical reports, postmortem reports and photographs. She is highly qualified in head injuries, both child and adult, and I believe her expertise is far superior to that of either Garrett or Freeman.

She began her report by stating her grave concern at Mandy's postmortem report, particularly the investigation of the head injury. As I mentioned earlier, the investigation into Mandy's head injuries had been zero from the fall at school in November 1990.

Helen says that Garrett did not perform the absolute necessities of a postmortem and had failed to carry out basic procedures. In children, she says, it is not necessary for there to be a skull fracture for subdural haematoma or brain haemorrhage to occur: it is well recognised that trivial injury can cause cerebral oedema and death and if cerebral oedema is present, it can be exacerbated by vomiting and/or fitting. Mandy had cerebral palsy and, therefore, was more likely than most to develop subdural haematomas. Helen concluded that the cause of Mandy's death was cerebral oedema with subdural haematoma. Direct trauma was the most likely cause of the head injury. Shaking is almost always restricted to the infantile age group.

I wept when I read this report. It showed that what Les and I had said was the truth and now it was coming out. I thought of how Garrett and Freeman must be made to answer for what they had done and said: Freeman because of his glaring absence during Mandy's health problems and Garrett because of his failure to conduct a postmortem properly.

Campbell sent a copy of Helen's report to Philip Wrightson. And then I had to wait for the next step along the route to freedom.

CHAPTER
························
8

WHAT WAS WAKEFIELD prison really like? Like hell is my answer to that question. It is still difficult for me to believe that so-called human beings can treat their fellows in the ways I have witnessed. The screws are bent on causing as much grief as possible. Prison works, the public are continually told. Bullshit, I say to that. The screws have little, if any, interest in prisoners or their rights. If you could see the way they group together when the riot bell goes, then you would see just how keen they are to wade in at any one of us. I know. I've seen it.

The riot bell went on our wing one day. An Irish lad, Tony, complained about the food and was greeted with the usual verbal abuse from the kitchen screws. This annoyed him so he tipped the gravy container over the floor. Screws came running and booted the shit out of him. He wasn't posing any threat but he got it from every screw. Some of us tried to help him but the screws blocked off all the routes to where he was so that they could carry on unimpeded. I would estimate that around forty screws were beating Tony. Weren't they brave? Maybe this is the new regime that the Government wants to put in place when it tells the public that prisons are too soft. Tell that to Tony.

More often than not the answer to any question is no; the answer to any request is no. If an inmate makes a complaint, the prison is always right and the inmate always wrong. Inmates are put in the punishment block for the most minor infringements of rules. I was sent there for wearing my own T-shirt at dinner-time, for standing on a rail, for refusing to accept legal papers relating to my children's case. Each time I was judged guilty as charged.

The food is always poor quality. Everything starts with the premise that costs must be cut at the prisoners' expense. However, if anyone of note comes into the prison a luxurious buffet is put on, the screws have their own buffet and, all of a sudden, the media are yelling that the inmates receive amazing food. The show lasts until the visitor leaves. A good example of what goes on when a prison is in the spotlight happened in 1994 when TV cameras came into Wakefield. As soon as the screws saw them they jumped off their idle arses and mingled with inmates, chatting away. I looked down from my landing and saw dozens of friendly screws, and thought, What a load of two-faced bastards. As soon as the cameras went, the screws sat back down like clockwork. That's called leading the public to a false perception. Normality goes haywire the moment a prisoner gets to reception. The attitude is: Put them in a striped shirt and forget about them.

I have seen how suicides are viewed in prison. A mate of mine had problems with his girlfriend. He asked for help but was refused. One night he went behind his door in a good mood, or so we thought. The following morning when the screws came round to check that we were all still there, I heard one shout, 'One's swinging.' My mate had hanged himself and this bastard saw it as a joke.

Not long after I arrived at this hell-hole, I was appointed a personal officer. I told him about the case, he told me that as a screw, 'I can't get involved.' They hid behind this limp excuse when and as it suited them. Some months later this screw came to me and said, 'We've got reports to do, Kev.' I said to him, 'I can't get involved.' His face was a picture. When one is sentenced – rightly or wrongly – a series of reports is compiled by the personal officer. The reports, which are mandatory, are based on issues such as offending behaviour, remorse and attending certain courses all aimed at dealing with guilt. I took no part in any of this farce as I was an innocent victim of this very system. I made this abundantly clear to my personal officer right from the beginning and because of this I was tagged as being a subversive. All they were concerned about was completing their reports on me and totally ignoring the fact that they were dealing with an innocent man.

Another example of my treatment in Wakefield was when a wing governor called me to his office and told me that he had to serve some papers on me. He told me that he had read the legal papers which he had in his hand. The papers were concerning my children. If I signed them it meant that I agreed to the adoption of my son, a matter which I have had no say in to this present day. It was bad enough being in that prison as an innocent man, without losing my son too. I told him that I was not accepting papers from him or anyone else and that I would not sign for them either and walked out. He shouted me back but I went to my cell. The same night I received a nicking sheet and was put in the punishment block the following morning, where I was found guilty as charged. It mattered not that they had no legal right to even attempt to act as bailiffs, they still found me guilty.

Even though we were making such headway with my case, I still had to contend with such absurdities at Wakefield prison. They tried to make me attend courses, one of which was to address offending behaviour. I asked the screw to what offending behaviour he was referring. He couldn't answer me but replied that the course would be good for me! What they wanted was for me to pack in my fight. Prison staff at

Wakefield hate inmates who contest their convictions and saw me as though I was fighting *them*. What they couldn't understand was that they had nothing to do with my wrongful conviction. It didn't matter what I told them, or showed them, they still wanted me to bow down and 'conform', but I could never do that. Because I had not committed any crime. Not one screw ever said to me, 'We have concerns about your conviction and would like to assist you.' All they ever said was, 'We can't get involved.'

I had it rammed down my throat in prison that rules must be obeyed. But these rules did not allow for me to contest a wrongful conviction and caused me huge problems. No one ever stopped to think that I might actually be innocent as I said I was. They read every letter that I received or sent, thus preventing me from corresponding properly with my legal and medical team. (I had to hand mail to my sister, Janice, to stop the screws reading it.) Obstacles were placed in my way all down the line.

It is only quite recently that prisoners have been allowed to use a phone at dinner-time – if the screws agree to put one in. How, then, are innocent people supposed to keep in contact with their legal advisers? One day I spoke to a pathologist who had studied the evidence in my case and was firmly on my side. I asked the prison authorities for a copy of the taped recording of my conversation but they said no. I explained that the call contained strong evidence of my innocence but they still said no. All I wanted was the right to contest my conviction unhindered but apparently this was too much to ask. I wrote to Derek Lewis, the director-general of prisons, and told him of all the barriers I was running into. He wrote back saying, 'The sooner you settle into prison life the easier it will be.'

One day Campbell came to see me, bringing the news that the evidence of Paul Weir and Steven Hague had now been categorically 'disproved' – a polite way of saying that their evidence had been fabrication. He said he was going to try to speed up the process to the appeal hearing as the prosecution no longer had a case against me. Luckily for me, Campbell had kept the Court of Appeal informed of what was going on with my case from a very early stage and they had been very courteous to us – in fact, the Registrar had indicated that in July 1993 there had been enough evidence for appeal and that my barrister should be advised to take this step.

On 4 March 1994 Campbell brought the full, perfected grounds of appeal to show me. They had been submitted to the Court of Appeal and served direct on the prosecution. He also brought me an article which was to appear in the Manchester *Evening News* that night. He asked if I could make a phone call when I got back to the wing. Why, I asked. 'Because the BBC would like to interview you for tonight's edition of the main news,' he replied. I would try, I told him, but he, too, knew how I was treated. He handed all the papers over to me – but only after he'd had to get permission to do so from the screws. Great, isn't it? My own case, my wrongful conviction and my own solicitor, and he had to have permission to give me what was rightly mine.

I got back to the wing on a high, only to be brought down to earth by a screw. I asked if I could make a call. He asked me my name. I told him that that was not the issue, the issue was that I had asked for a call. He repeatedly asked for my name until it really got up my nose. 'Mickey fucking mouse,' I replied, and went up to see if the legal aid screw was in. He was and I told him about trying to get a call out and the response I had had from the screw on the wing. 'Yes, by all means, call the people you want to speak to,' he said. His name was Gary Smith and he was the only person in the prison who had a genuine interest in my case.

I got through to the BBC and was interviewed there and then by a woman called Morven Williams. She asked me how I felt after seeing my solicitor and being told of the great news. I just let go with sheer emotion, praised my whole team, and said how pleased I was that all my hard work had borne fruit.

I wasn't prepared for the large-scale coverage of this one call. That night Campbell appeared on the television, blowing my trumpet for grasping the complex issue of the case. It was on every TV news bulletin that night and also on the radio.

The evidence we had submitted could not be challenged by the prosecution and I saw no reason for any delay to my freedom being granted by the Court of Appeal, but I had to wait for the Single Judge to grant me leave to appeal. My family had been overjoyed at the news they had received from me and Campbell.

However, on Friday, 15 April 1994 – the third anniversary of Mandy's death – I was handed a letter from a legal aid screw. I went into my cell and read it. It was from the Single Judge at the Court of Appeal. Much to my horror, Judge Tucker refused leave to appeal. He said that this new evidence should have been called at trial and that he would not have granted an appeal in any event. 'The fact that two new experts have now been found does not entitle you to reopen matters in my opinion,' he concluded.

I couldn't believe what I was reading. If the evidence submitted to Judge Tucker had been *available* at trial then I would not have been convicted. The strongest appeal to be submitted is one of 'fresh evidence', and mine was solely based on that issue.

I phoned Campbell and told him what I'd just read. He was livid that this ruling by Judge Tucker had been sent direct to me. He had told the Court of Appeal to contact him first and he would then inform me of their verdict. I felt sick thinking that, by some horrible coincidence, I had received the news on that particular day, and I said so to Campbell. He said, 'Kevin, don't worry, we'll get there. It would be a travesty of justice if we weren't granted leave to appeal,' and went on to voice his own disgust at what Judge Tucker had said. He told me that all case papers would be resubmitted to three judges.

In spite of Campbell's attempts to reassure me, I felt very

depressed. It seemed like we were almost back at the beginning, having to resubmit the papers. Shit, I thought, not again, and the waiting, the worry, the stress all hit me hard.

I saw Campbell again on 12 May 1994. He was still confident that we would get leave to appeal and that my conviction would be overturned. It was a great boost to my morale and even more so on Monday, 16 May when he told me that the Crown Prosecution Service had instructed Professor Michael Green to study the medical evidence from my trial. Michael Green is a forensic pathologist based in Sheffield with whom I had previously corresponded and who had dealt with a case in which the allegation against the accused was the same as that made against me. In that case, however, it had been shown that shock waves and not shaking had been responsible for the death. So I felt relaxed at Professor Green acting for the prosecution.

On 21 May, I had a letter from Campbell telling me that he had been talking to Helen Whitwell who had discussed my case with Professor Bernard Knight, a leading expert in forensic pathology. Professor Knight had expressed interest in my case when I had first contacted the Royal College of Pathologists – indeed, it had been he who had first told me that Garrett's and Freeman's evidence at my trial was worthy of challenge. Helen was sure that Professor Knight would support her opinion that shaking had not been what caused Mandy's death. She added that she would also talk to David Graham, who was based at Glasgow University and came very highly recommended from Philip Wrightson. She also talked to Professor Green about her anxiety over Garrett's and Freeman's conclusions and made it clear that the evidence at trial could not possibly be relied upon. Professor Green responded, 'It is necessary for standards to be improved and maintained.' Many experts of world repute were involved in my case and medical opinion of Garrett's and Freeman's conclusions and opinions was openly adverse.

*

I was still getting heavy treatment from the screws in Wakefield. During one week in the latter part of 1994 I was subjected to three cell searches. They rifled my legal papers, even though I said they were strictly confidential, so I complained to the governor. As usual, this fell on deaf ears, so I complained to Campbell who sent a strongly worded letter to the governor telling him that his staff had no right to go through my legal papers.

On one of these searches the screw came out of my cell with two pieces of wire which I had never seen. The next day I was put in the punishment block. I asked to speak to my solicitor because, first, the cell search had been illegal: I had not been allowed to be there while it was carried out and the door was pushed to so that I could not see what was going on. Also, the wires must have been planted by someone. The governor, however, told me that I could not contact Campbell and that I was guilty as charged. He fined me and took my radio off me for a month.

Campbell, though, sent me a copy of the letter he had sent to the governor: it told him to leave my legal documentation alone and to stop the victimisation that was evident. If it went on, he would take legal action on my behalf. It stopped.

But what was happening with the resubmission of my case to the three judges at the Appeal Court? I soon found out. We were granted an oral hearing to apply for leave to appeal, which Michael Mansfield QC was to argue on my behalf. The date set for the hearing was 31 October and Campbell went too. He said he'd tell his office the outcome and they would fax it to me. Both my lawyers were confident but I still had Judge Tucker's words ringing in my ears. At around 4.10 p.m. on the thirty-first, as promised, I received a fax: 'Congratulations, leave granted.' I was thrilled to bits.

The news of this success filtered through to the Manchester *Evening News* and my local paper, which said the full appeal would probably be heard in early 1995. I don't know where they got that from but it appeared.

Campbell also thought that the appeal would be heard early in 1995. First, though, the prosecution wanted to discuss my case with their own neurosurgeon. This was absurd, as far as I was concerned, as the defence had already secured two leading experts on head injury in children. Still, if they wanted to go ahead then they could. They would come back with nothing but what we already knew.

I received a copy of the transcript from the oral hearing, which had been held before Their Honours Justices Harrison, Leggatt and Latham. They were critical of the prosecution evidence, both medical and otherwise, and stated that it would be expedient in the interests of justice for Helen Whitwell's evidence to be heard and added that, irrespective of whether or not there had been a good reason to omit this evidence at my trial, they had no hesitation in granting me leave to appeal. What a change from Tucker's absurdities. These three judges had concluded that all the experts now involved were agreed that the medical evidence responsible for my conviction was flawed and unjust.

On 9 December 1994 I saw Campbell, who was certain there was no possibility of the prosecution challenging our case. However, before we could proceed, we had to wait for a report being compiled by the prosecution expert, Myles Gibson, a neurosurgeon based in Leeds. The prosecution were to hold a conference on 19 December to discuss what they were going to do. There wasn't much they could do, and we heard that they had agreed it would be difficult to sustain the conviction. The first entry in my 1995 diary is, 'Go for full truth and freedom.'

Myles Gibson's report seemed to take an eternity to come through and Campbell pressed the prosecution to get on with it, but nothing was forthcoming until February. In the meantime, though, I was getting seriously depressed. I couldn't take much more of the stress of waiting and it seemed like the prosecution were deliberately stretching my – and my team's – patience. The secretaries at Campbell's office, Linda Harrison especially, must have got fed up of me calling so often. I poured my heart out to her on one occasion. Maybe I shouldn't have done but who else could I have turned to?

I also made contact with Les, to tell her that I was going to send her the evidence we were going to present. That way, I thought, she wouldn't be so shocked to learn exactly how Mandy had died. The cause of her death had definitely not been as alleged at trial and I believed that Les, as Mandy's mother, had the right to know how Mandy died. I typed it all out myself and mailed if off but received no reply – much to my amazement.

We finally had some news on 17 February. I spoke to Linda, who told me that we had received a choice of eight dates for appeal, and that the first was Monday, 27 March. However, we couldn't go ahead because Myles Gibson's report still wasn't through. I was fed up with the endless delays. I spoke to Linda again on 6 March. She was very excited about something.

'Kevin,' she said, 'did you get the fax?'

'No,' I replied.

'I'll put you through to Campbell,' and off she went.

Campbell came on. 'Where's the fax?' he asked.

'I've received no fax,' I replied.

'Well, it was a fax of the report from Myles Gibson,' he said, and read out its main content.

'Jesus, Campbell, it's the end of the case, isn't it?' I said, hardly daring to believe it.

'Yes, the case is now over, collapsed,' he said.

Can I explain how I felt at the news? No way. I was ecstatic and whooping for joy, yes, but I was – if this is understandable – also sad, even though all my hard work had paid off.

When I finished work that day, I went to the wing office and asked if there was a fax for me. No reply came but a hand

passed it to me. I walked away, reading the damn thing as fast
as I could. Back you go to your cell, boy, I told myself, and get
composed. I sat in the cell and read it, noticing that they'd
kept page one away from me. I will quote the main areas of
Myles Gibson's report to give the reader a glimpse of how the
prosecution now viewed this case.

My opinion would be that on the information available to
us this child (four years of age) sustained a blunt injury to
the head and developed cerebral oedema and subdural
haematoma collections. These resulted in raised intracranial pressure which in turn led to respiratory difficulties.
There could have been some additional factor contributing
to the intracranial pressure when hypoxia developed if there
was inhalation of vomit.

Closed head injury in children can present in distressing
and misleading ways in that the initial condition may appear
to be satisfactory, only for a severe form of brain oedema to
develop within a matter of hours. This may be preceded by
headache or drowsiness or just general distress.

Retinal haemorrhages are not exclusively caused by shaking events and this girl was outside the age which one
associates with retinal haemorrhages due to shaking, even
making allowance for the fact that she suffered from a form
of cerebral palsy and had mild ventricular dilatation. On the
balance of probability I feel it would be unlikely that the
retinal haemorrhages and the subdural collections were
occasioned by shaking and I believe in her case the brain
swelling and the subdural collections were a result of a
blunt closed injury to the head. Once the physiopatholog-
ical process has been set in train the development of brain
swelling and brain oedema can be enhanced by vomiting,
difficulty with the airway and hypoxia. Since the clinical
condition of this girl in the hour or two immediately prior
to her death is not recorded we will never be able to determine the exact nature of her clinical pathological events.

On balance however I would feel that the findings in this girl's head were not the result of shaking.

P.S. Since dictating this report a leading British medical journal has published an editorial annotation on the shaken baby. There is nothing in it to make me change my opinion as given above but perhaps more importantly it states clearly that the shaken baby syndrome is extremely rare after the age of two years and this is in line with my own experience.

I called Linda and let out a whoop of joy so loud that everyone gawped at me as if I'd gone mad. She whooped with me, then said she'd be making sure that my team were all available to go ahead on 27 March. Obviously this had to be subject to the prosecution getting their fingers out, which so far they had not done. I called my family that evening and they, too, were overjoyed. Everyone was now expecting me to be out before Easter 1995.

I couldn't be completely happy, though, even now. The prosecution were still dragging their heels. I hated all the waiting. After all, they had approached two experts, Professor Green and Myles Gibson, to analyse all the medical evidence from the case and they had stated that Mandy had not died as alleged at my trial. Therefore, what evidence could possibly be forthcoming from the prosecution? But it was worrying and stressful for me. I had to try to occupy my mind elsewhere, if I could. None of my legal team was in any doubt as to the outcome of the appeal and I phoned them often, just to hear their reassuring voices. I honestly don't know how Linda Harrison has coped with me over these years. She has been a darling in her support and understanding, as have the other secretaries. To have this whole team behind me gave me a very secure feeling and I firmly believe that when an innocent man is contesting his conviction, it is vital that the legal team has a good insight into what it is like to be locked up for something you haven't done. I was so lucky to have Campbell Malone, a staunch campaigner in miscarriages of justice, on my side.

I kept in touch with Les's parents, although Les was still ignoring me. In the end, I stopped all contact with Les and her parents. I did, however, continue to try to support other people in similar positions to my own. Sue May's name sticks out the most. One thing my case has left me with is a burning desire to help people like Sue and I would like to play an active part in the future in detecting miscarriages of justice. And another positive thing is that I enjoyed uncovering the truth of my own wrongful conviction. It taught me so much about pathology, the way in which the legal system works and how to formulate a challenge to a conviction. It has also shown me how much the prison system hates people who make such challenges . . .

On 15 March 1995, I saw my parents at Wakefield for the last time. My brother, Keith, came with them. It was so good to know that the case was almost over. All we needed now was a date, but the prosecution was still making sure that a date could not be fixed. That week, though, the Court of Appeal phoned Campbell's office to say that if the prosecution did not oppose the appeal we could go ahead on 10 April. Campbell put pressure on the prosecution to come up with some answers and was finally told that the CPS would inform him of their way forward on 27 March.

At 4.10 p.m. on Monday, 27 March 1995, a call came through for me on the wing screw's phone from my solicitors. It was Linda Harrison. 'We've had a response from the CPS and I'll read it to you,' she said. '"We do not oppose any bail application and we will not be resisting the appeal."' I screamed with delight. The screw thought I'd gone crackers. I held on to the phone for as long as I could. Linda was really chuffed for me and I asked her to send me a copy of the letter from the CPS and to call my parents to let them know. When we said good-bye, I told the screw what had happened. He actually seemed rather pleased for me! I couldn't apply for bail because it was too near to the appeal date but not even that could take away my joy.

Later, when I called my parents myself, Mam answered the phone. She simply said, 'Well.'

I whooped for joy at her. 'Mam,' I said, 'this is it, it's all over now.' We were like kids in our happiness but I couldn't care less how I was – I was over the moon that we'd done it, at long last. I told Mam I didn't care about the bail not being possible. The main thing was that the prosecution had now realised that I, Kevin John Callan, had been wrongly convicted for a crime that never took place. I gained two things from this: one was joy, the other pain at what people had done to Mandy. All the prosecution witnesses had a lot to answer for now, I thought.

CHAPTER

· · · · · · · · · · · · · · · ·

9

I WENT TO bed that night with a million and one things running through my mind. I nodded off only to find myself wide awake at about 5.30 a.m. I got up, made a brew and sat on the edge of my bed. I reflected on the pain and trauma that I, and everyone else involved, had been through over the last four years, Mandy uppermost in my mind. I thought about my family, that we would soon be reunited. A thrill surged through me. I felt absolutely knackered after four years of continuous fight but I was definitely going home; no one in Wakefield could do a fucking thing about it – much as they'd have liked to – and the nightmare was over.

Later on that day, I went to see Paul Laxton, the screw in charge of work, and told him that I wouldn't be going to work again as I needed time to come to terms with what was happening to me. He agreed, and I stayed off work. I'd given three years' excellent work service and I reckoned I'd done my fair share. I'd been paid a whopping £8.75 per week as a painter, redecorating the wings and cells. I did the prison course, which enabled me to do a competent job.

Needless to say, the pay structure did not reflect the standard of work produced. We all tried to get decent pay for the work we put in but the prison governor would have none of it. He said no funds were available for a better pay structure. Utter bollocks. He had plenty of money to spend on a locker room for the screws, an Astroturf football pitch and tree-planting.

I had no intention of turning out for work, whatever Paul Laxton said, but even though he had agreed that I needn't go it didn't stop the screws locking me behind a cell door all day long. I asked Paul Laxton if it could be left open as I was now a proven innocent man but he said no, the door had to be locked. I feel sorry for folk having to face similar situations to the one I was in. With this sort of attitude, is it any wonder that it takes years to undo a wrongful conviction? The whole process of dealing with victims of alleged wrongful convictions, for whom there is a glaring lack of assistance, needs to be addressed urgently. In Wakefield, the governor made some absurd rulings: a phone call to your legal adviser is not allowed unless it is urgent. But who should determine whether or not a call is urgent? Who should decide on 27 March 1995 how urgent it was for me to call my solicitors? Luckily for me, my solicitors called me. They already knew I wouldn't have been allowed to call them.

There is no help in jail for an innocent man. It is like being raped of all rights, even though prisoners are not supposed to lose their civil rights. Let me tell you that a prisoner loses everything the moment he enters the prison. They make damn sure of that.

I hated Wakefield so much, everything about it. I see no reason why genuine people who challenge a wrongful conviction can't be helped. How do they judge when someone is genuine? Easy. By the amount of progress that person makes. I am only too aware that many appeals are based on flimsy evidence. But others stand on firm ground. It is quite easy to tell when someone is telling the truth from the number of times their story changes. My experience has enabled me to clock very quickly if someone has a genuine case or not.

Just as she said she would, Linda sent me a copy of the CPS's letter to the Court of Appeal. It reads:

The Registrar

Dear Sirs,
Re: R *v.* Kevin Callan
Appeal Number T94/1614/Y3

Further to my conversation with you last week, I now write to inform you that in the light of an Advice given by Mr Henriques of Counsel the Prosecution have decided today not to resist the Appeal against Conviction made by Mr Callan. In these circumstances the Prosecution would not oppose any Application for Bail made by Mr Callan. I have forwarded a copy of this letter to the Solicitors for Mr Callan who will no doubt wish the case to be listed as soon as possible.
Yours faithfully,
R.A. Davies
Branch Crown Prosecutor

Seeing it in black and white meant far more to me than when I heard it over the phone. I showed it to the wing screw, who told me he was really happy for me and I sent a copy to my parents. Next day, 29 March, I sent a heartfelt thank-you card to the secretaries, especially Linda, at Campbell's office. We had now been told that the Court of Appeal would like the case heard on 6 April, two days before my birthday. Nice one! What a brilliant day it was turning out to be.

That afternoon, however, I was in my cell writing my story when a screw opened the door and told me to go to work. I told him that Paul Laxton had given me permission to stay away. He said, 'I don't give a shit what he said, I'm giving you a direct order.'

'Shove it,' I said. He shut the door and I couldn't have cared less. This was my joy, and I wanted my privacy to come to terms with the events of the last few days. It was not to be. Around four o'clock the doors were opened. The same screw was shouting his head off at someone. I yelled to him, 'Why don't you nick him?'

He said, 'If you've got anything to say, get down here and say it.'

I didn't need any more prompting. 'I've now been proven innocent and you fucking bastards just won't leave me alone for my last few days. Fuck off, you shower of bastards,' I said.

At eight, two screws came into my cell and gave me two 'nicking sheets', one for refusing a direct order, the other for using foul and abusive language. The following morning I was hauled off to the punishment block and appeared before one of the governors. In front of him I appeared to enjoy the rubbish the screws were coming out with. 'How do you plead to the charges?' I was asked.

'I just want to be left alone as the case against me has now officially collapsed,' I said. 'I asked P O Laxton if I could stay off until I am released and he said yes.'

'Is this true?' he said.

'Yes,' I replied. 'I cleared it with him on two occasions, the latter being when I actually showed him the fax from the CPS not objecting to bail or opposing the appeal.' I asked the governor if I was expecting too much in wanting time to myself to come to terms with what was happening to me.

'Oh, we'll give you that, all right,' he said. 'Three days' cellular confinement.' This meant I had to spend three days in the 'block'. No cigarettes, no calls to my legal advisers, no papers, nothing. And this on the day my case made national headlines. I just hope that the governor now feels as embarrassed as he should.

What a horrendous place the block is. I was stripped of my

clothes and two screws with me demanded that I had a shower. Afterwards, they made me put prison clothing on; strictly punishment in itself. Then I went back to a cell to be locked in.

Later, they called me for a visit. Janice and Keith had come but were not allowed to see me in the communal visiting area. Instead I was put in a little room with three screws. When Keith and Janice came in, Keith saw straight away that something was wrong. 'What's going on here?' he said.

'I'm being punished because I have proved my innocence,' I said. Tempers flared and the visit was wrecked before it had begun. The screws even tried to stop me having a fag and one screw openly threatened to do me in when I got back to my cell. He didn't do but they treated me like a caged animal. I was unaware that my case was causing a big stir out in the real world. The screws wouldn't even speak to me and I got no food or liquids from them during my stay in the block. Time dragged and I couldn't sleep. I just lay on the bed that was bolted to the floor. I remember one morning they brought a lad into the block. I heard him scream for his life, which took me straight back to the beating I had received at the Bridewell. Tears came to my eyes as I heard him.

Sunday came, and I was due back on the wing. They brought a bucket with a rag, told me to clean the cell, which I did. Then a screw turned up with my wing clothes. 'Fuck the clothes,' I said, 'where's my fags?' I had my trousers half down my legs and there I was looking for my fags.

'I'll come back later for you,' he said, and locked me back in.

He'd also given me some mail, so I lit a fag up and started to read. Suddenly I went very dizzy and had to sit down quick. It was comforting to get mail after three days of nothing, though.

A short while later the screw came to take me back to the wing. Thank God for that, I thought. Off we went – and the mood changed. This screw began telling me of the publicity about my case. One minute he had this hard image, the next he's treating me like he's known me for years. He told me that it had been in all the papers, on the TV and that Campbell had given an interview on TV too.

By this time we were back in the centre of the prison and I saw D Wing with relief. I was let on to the wing to be greeted with a message. 'Can you phone your mam and dad and can you phone Keith?' When I spoke to them, they were full of how big the case was. Then people on the wing suddenly got wind that I was back and were coming up to tell me all about the case being on TV and in the papers. The atmosphere was brilliant. The lads on the wing were over the moon for me that I'd taken on the might of the legal and medical professions. More than anything, I suppose, I'd shown them that they, too, if they were in a position like mine, could prove their own innocence.

When I read the mail I'd been given in the block earlier, one letter stuck out from the rest. Dr Dossett's widow had written to say she was elated to hear the news about me. Her husband had recently died from cancer. She told me that he had been sorry that he could not become directly involved with my case due to his illness. He firmly believed in my innocence, she said. She told me that she had actually been standing beside him while I was talking to him. I was so touched that Mrs Dossett had taken the trouble to write to me, and especially at such a sad time for her.

Another moving letter came from Gloucester from a lady who had been suffering from a head injury for many years. So far she had only been treated by an osteopath so I suggested she contact some of the neurosurgeons with whom I had become acquainted. Other mail came from members of the general public and the press with their congratulations.

I desperately needed some sleep. I was knackered after my ordeal on the block so I went and had a shower, collected my paper and some more mail. This time there was a card from Mam and Dad:

Well done, Kevin. Dad and I are so proud of you and are looking forward to Thursday, 6 April. Yippee. See you then. All our love,
Mam and Dad.
We love you.

What a lovely surprise. I love them both.

Monday, 4 April arrived, and I'd still had virtually no sleep. The case was beginning to get to me and more so because of the press coverage it had been attracting. It was impossible for me to grasp quite how widespread press interest had been because I hadn't been allowed to see any of it while I was in the block. However, I spoke to Linda Harrison at dinner-time and she told me that all the media wanted interviews. I told her I couldn't respond to anyone until I had spoken to Campbell. As my immediate and legal adviser, his advice would dictate the pattern of the next few days. Then Campbell himself came on the line and asked me how I was doing. He's so cool at times like this. He told me how to deal with the media and I'm mighty pleased he did. I took his advice right along the line. He'd been through it all before and I hadn't. I asked him to take full control of all the publicity on the understanding that he stayed with me through it all. He agreed to this without hesitation and said he'd try to see me before the appeal if he could find time. He told me that I would be up before one of the judges who granted me leave to appeal, which made me feel good. We talked about giving a press statement after my release too, but it wasn't until we discussed the TV programmes that wanted me to appear that it hit home to me just how large-scale the publicity about my appeal had become.

'Campbell, I'm not prepared for all this,' I told him, but he only laughed and told me I'd be OK.

I got no sleep that night either and stayed awake listening to chat-shows. In the morning I had to see a doctor to report fit for travel. All that happened was that he scribbled F.F.T. across a piece of paper after asking me if I was OK. No physical examination, nothing but that one question.

I also learnt, that Tuesday, and much to my pleasure, that Securicor had taken over running security at the Court of Appeal, which meant that the screws would not be permitted to be in the dock with me for the hearing. However, the Prison Service hadn't liked this. They had been asked to assist in court duties but had refused. Nothing like stirring it up.

That day, too, I began to realise that the big one was here. It turned my stomach with excitement. It was a lovely feeling. All the lads wished me the best. Even the screws treated me differently. They were talking to me even whereas, before, they had no time for me. Screws are quick to make their own judgements based on what they read in a prisoner's file, which does not contain one iota of fresh evidence that may have materialised since conviction.

Wednesday morning finally came and my cell door was unlocked earlier than usual. Today I was going to London. I was all packed and ready. I was asked if I would like to go and have a shower. Off I went for a good soak, then back to my cell to prepare for departure and gather my few remaining belongings. I made sure that I had enough tobacco to last me until after the appeal. I couldn't face breakfast and instead had a brew. I said my goodbyes to the lads, especially the ones who had given me a parting 'gift' the previous night: a plastic carrier bag which they said contained a cake. When I opened it, it was to discover several manky old socks . . . They also got me a card, which they'd all signed along with their comical messages of congratulations, which was real nice.

Then it was time to go and meet up with the two screws who were taking me to Brixton where I would spend the night before the appeal. I picked up some stuff and we headed for the gates of D Wing. The lads gave me a good send off, as did everyone on the other wings who were watching my departure.

Out through the big horrible iron gates we strode and we were soon at reception. I had to go through all my property record again. They let me keep the tobacco I had in my tin and told me I would be given more and anything else I needed when I got to Brixton.

The formalities were over and it was time for handcuffs: two pairs, one cuff on each wrist and a screw attached to the other on either side. Then, not content with clapping two sets of handcuffs on an innocent man, they went through the serious routine of checking that they had been put on properly. This could only be done by another officer. What a waste of resources. Why couldn't the screw who put them on check them? Their crazy attitude never failed to amaze me. Eventually we were 'cleared' and got into a private taxi, drove through the security barriers and out on to the road. When the last set of prison gates opened, I felt a weight lift as I left that place for ever.

CHAPTER

· · · · · · · · · · · · · · · ·

10

TRYING TO HAVE a smoke clamped to two other people is a joke, to say the least, but in spite of the cramped conditions I talked to the screws about my appeal. They had no doubt that my release was a foregone conclusion. It was, though, one shitty journey.

Along the way to Brixton, I asked the two screws to make sure that I was handed my tobacco and wash-kit once I was in the prison, which they said they would do. Things did not work out this way. We arrived at Brixton at about two o'clock in the afternoon. I had arranged for someone to come and see me on a visit once I had arrived at Brixton but the screws there would have none of it, saying it was too late for any visit to take place. Fuck the lot of you then, you shower of bastards, I thought.

When I went through reception they searched and then strip-searched me. Once I had got dressed I asked for my tobacco and wash-kit. 'You can't have them as they're sealed up with the rest of your property,' I was told.

After I had been processed I was taken to a wing and told to go to the landing office. Once there I gave the screws a card that had been stuck in my hand at reception. I was then taken to a cell, where I was greeted by filthy, useless bedding, rubbish on the floor, days-old food scattered about and plastic cutlery green with mould.

I tried to get a brew sorted out but the screws told me that they had no cups, tea-bags, sugar or milk for the prisoners. I asked if I could make some phone calls to be told that I could make one only because I had not pre-booked a call. I'd only just arrived so how I was supposed to have done that is something I still have difficulty in understanding to this day.

I phoned the person who had arranged to visit me that day, Sylvie Carswell, a good friend of Judy Ward. As a teenager, Judy Ward was found guilty of the infamous M62 bombing of an army coach. She spent sixteen years in prison as yet another innocent victim of our judiciary. Sylvie told me that she had phoned the prison several times only to be told that I was not known to Brixton and was not there. Sylvie had been to see me in Wakefield and she and Judy gave me cracking support. I phoned her quite often to keep her up to date with what was going on in the case. She and Judy, she said, had organised a reception for after my release.

After we hung up I tried again to get a brew – it was a complete waste of time. Later, when I was being locked up for the night, I asked the screw for a toothbrush, some toothpaste, a comb and a towel but, 'No,' he said, 'we don't have any of that up here.' I had to spend the night without tobacco, brew, food and something to read. After what seemed an eternity, I managed to drop off to sleep, much to my surprise. Considering what was to happen next day I did well to get any sleep at all.

When I woke in the morning, the cell door was unlocked and I went to splash my face with cold water then went downstairs and joined a bunch of lads who were all going somewhere that day. Those of us destined for the Court of Appeal were kept together, and the others were grouped according to which court they were attending. Some were being released after serving their sentences. One by one we were called to identify our belongings. Next we had to strip off in a cubicle and our clothing was searched. Then, at last, I was shown to a hatch in the wall where I got a brew of tea containing sugar – sheer bliss – and told to go to a 'holding area', which consisted of some cells larger than the ones on the wings, each labelled for the various courts individuals would be attending. I wanted the one labelled 'Court of Appeal'. In I went and sat down with my much-needed tea. Other lads destined for the Court soon followed me in, each with their brew. As we waited for transport we got talking about our cases. I told them what I was appealing against and one lad said he had seen my case on TV last week and also last night. They asked how I had put up with prison, knowing all along I was innocent. Easy, I said, I always knew that one day I would be freed because I was genuinely innocent. How does it feel to know that you're only a few hours away from freedom? I was asked. 'Very exciting,' I said. Their reaction was warming and comforting and helped me relax a bit.

'Right, lads,' came a shout from a guy dressed in a Securicor outfit.

One by one we were handcuffed and put into this new Securicor van. Inside, it contained small cells, better known as sweatboxes because of their minimum light, air and room. I could see out of the window of mine but nobody could see into the van. To the right of me was the Securicor guard. He switched on a radio, which we could all hear as speakers were fitted along the roof. Well, this is it now, I thought. The next stop is the big one. I felt excitement and nerves at the same time. My stomach turned over at the thought of what lay ahead of us. I tried to concentrate on listening to the radio but my mind wandered all over the show as each gear-change brought us closer to the Court of Appeal.

Suddenly I saw a sign which read 'Strand'. Oh, shit, I thought, we're almost there. Then I spotted a building, which was obviously of some importance, but as a few photographers were outside it I reckoned it couldn't be the court building. But then came the sign, 'The Royal Courts of Justice'. We swung wide into the road and turned left into a spacious yard. Cameras were being stuck at the van's windows and flashes were going off, one at my window. I don't have a clue if the photo came out.

The van backed up tight to a door, through which each of us was taken, one by one, until it was empty. I was taken to a desk, gave my name, and was then put into a large room with a few others. No sooner had I got there than the two screws from Wakefield appeared.

'Where have you been?' they asked.

'I've only just got here,' I replied.

'Where's your suit?' one asked.

'It's here somewhere,' I replied.

They went out and quickly returned with my suit, tie, socks and shoes. 'Hurry up, it's time for you to go up now,' they said. I had to get dressed going up the stairs to the Court. When we got to the top, I straightened myself up as best I could under the circumstances.

Suddenly a large door swung open and I spun round to see, for the very first time, inside the Court of Appeal. What a sight for sore eyes. A Securicor fellow told me to enter the Court – but I still hadn't managed to do up my shoes and my tie was still loose. But it wasn't until I walked in that I saw the full scale of the courtroom. Oh, no, I thought, let this happen to someone else instead of me. I can't handle all these people gawping at me. I was told to sit on a long wooden bench. There was a Securicor man to the left of me and another to the right. The two Wakefield screws stood near the door where we came in.

I felt my legs turn to jelly when I saw that the three judges were already seated and looking pissed off because they had to hear this appeal. I began to shake: these awesome figures in red robes and white wigs frightened the life out of me. Then I saw my family: Janice and her daughter Joanne, Mam and

Dad, Keith and Lynn and another superb pair, Andrew Green of Conviction, and Judy Ward. Next I saw a lot of other people I had become friendly with over the past years: some were reporters who I had written to. As I scanned the public gallery, I saw that the people in it were there for my benefit. They had come to see justice done just as they would if it were one of their own family members who had been wrongly convicted. It was comforting to see them all: they'd all taken special time out to make the long trip to London from Manchester to be with me.

Directly facing me were reporters, all taking notes as soon as I appeared. Between them and me, though, I saw the best sight yet: Michael Mansfield QC, Jim Gregory – his junior barrister – and Campbell Malone. And lastly there was Linda Harrison, Campbell's secretary, up in the public gallery. Nice one, Linda, I thought to myself. I knew she had wanted to be at my appeal – she had put so much effort into it and the least she deserved was to witness a successful result for her efforts.

'Will the defendant please rise.' I got up and was asked if my name was Kevin John Callan.

'Yes,' I replied.

'Please be seated.' I nearly fell backwards off the bench.

Lord Justice Swinton Thomas opened the appeal hearing by asking Mr Henriques, prosecution QC, to outline the case.

'My Lords,' he began, 'this is a case in which the Crown does not oppose the appeal. We have formed the view that the overwhelming weight of material evidence supports the view that the injury was caused by trauma, not by shaking. That being so, we take the view that this conviction cannot be upheld.'

Lord Justice Swinton Thomas said, 'Yes, we have already formed that view ourselves.'

At this point I should have found myself relaxing. Instead, I shook even more. I pressed my feet against the panelled dock to try to calm myself. Needless to say, it did not do any good at all. I looked at the two screws from Wakefield: both were sticking their thumbs up. If anything, that unsettled me even more. The appeal was only a few minutes old and these two screws had grasped what the leading judge had said. I looked up to the public gallery where my family were smiling away at me.

On the appeal went. Lord Justice Swinton Thomas asked Mr Henriques to give a fuller account of the case as it was a case that was very much in the public eye. Mr Henriques gave a brief description of the events of 15 April 1991. As everyone else before him, he made no reference to the period between November 1990 and 15 April 1991, which was of critical importance as it was when Les and I had both seen the deterioration in Mandy's health, and nor to Mandy's having received insufficient care from the medical people who had given the 'evidence' at my trial responsible for me having spent the past four years in jail as a totally innocent person.

Mr Henriques went on, 'Dr Garrett's evidence, that the injuries must have been caused by shaking rather than direct trauma because there was no skull fracture, have been contradicted by every other doctor consulted.' He added that Professor Michael Green had made a report on behalf of the prosecution stating that Dr Garrett's evidence and handling of the postmortem had left a lot to be desired. When describing Garrett's involvement, Professor Green used phrases such as, 'impossible to justify', 'could well be challenged', 'inexcusable and absolute dogmatism'. There had been, Professor Green acknowledged, 'numerous regrettable breaches of protocol'. These comments are easy to understand when you remember that Dr Garrett – the crucial witness at my trial – was untrained in neurosurgery or neuropathy. Dr Freeman, the consultant paediatrician at my trial, was also lacking in such expertise.

Then it was time for Michael Mansfield to take the floor. Dressed in his black gown and white wig, he said, 'Based on the pathologist's evidence, police arrested Mr Callan and subjected him to forceful and severe questioning. This showed the dangers of a dogmatic approach to a defendant.' He continued, 'His first application for leave to appeal had been rejected. The court objected to him having, as the legal jargon put it, a second bite at the cherry. Had it not been for the applicant's persistence, this matter would not have taken this course . . . The case is a salutary lesson for the court system as none of the experts called at the original trial had the knowledge needed for the case.'

He told the court that Les had never believed I had killed her daughter in a fit of exasperation. Indeed, she had supported my appeal, and had given evidence at my trial that I was a devoted father figure, helping a severely disabled girl to learn to walk, talk and use a knife and fork. I had taught her how to bath herself and helped with her toilet training. He said that Les and I had planned to marry and had been about to move to Colwyn Bay, North Wales, when the tragedy happened.

Michael made many important points to the court but I firmly believe that the three vital ones were these:

There is a cautionary tale here both for the lawyers and the courts to ensure that expertise proffered to the jury is the proper one.

It is a sad reflection on the system that the miscarriage became clear only because of Mr Callan's persistence.

It is a sad reflection that it took Mr Callan himself to seek out the expert witnesses who got to the truth.

Michael had done an excellent job. We had far more evidence of a non-medical nature to fall back on if we needed it.

Now it was the judges' turn to comment upon the appeal hearing. Even though I knew that I would be released, there was still the fear at the back of my mind that something might stop it. It didn't happen like that though, quite the opposite.

Judge Swinton Thomas gave the court the full judgement, extracts of which I quote in the next passages.

Criticism is made . . . particularly of Dr Garrett and also, to an extent, of Dr Freeman . . . It is right to stress that from the outset the appellant has maintained that he is innocent, that he had always been very fond of children, that he never violently shook Amanda, and that he was wrongly convicted. He was, and is, as we have been told today, supported by Amanda's mother. He has worked tirelessly with a view to proving his innocence. To that end he has been greatly assisted by his solicitor, Mr Malone. We would wish to pay tribute to both of them. We would also pay tribute to the distinguished doctors who have assisted the defence and the Crown since the appellant's conviction.

Judge Swinton Thomas now turned to the experts' evidence, and first Helen Whitwell's. She had said, 'In my opinion direct trauma is by far the most likely cause of the head injury in this case than shaking.'

'In other words,' Judge Swinton Thomas went on, 'Dr Whitwell is saying that the explanation put forward by the appellant is far more likely than that put forward by the experts called for the Crown.' Then he turned to Philip Wrightson['s evidence]. 'Mr Wrightson is a distinguished neurosurgeon now living in New Zealand,' he said. 'He is in complete agreement with Dr Whitwell. Mr Wrightson says:

The cause of death was cerebral swelling and subdural haematoma. The original injury may have been relatively slight, but a second injury possibly, and vomiting, airway obstruction and hypoxia certainly, resulted in a very rapid onset of fatal changes. The injuries were not caused by shaking.'

Judge Swinton Thomas continued, 'Dr Whitwell and Mr Wrightson are very critical of Dr Garrett. Those criticisms are supported by Professor Green, the well-known and distinguished Professor of Forensic Pathology of the University of Sheffield, who has reported on this case for the Crown. The Crown also instructed Mr Myles Gibson, the distinguished neurological surgeon, who concluded, on balance, that Amanda's death did not result from shaking. Dr Garrett and Dr Freeman have both made further statements. To an extent, Dr Garrett has retreated from the original position taken by him at the trial. It is important, as Mr Mansfield has stressed in his submissions this morning, that experts with the correct expertise should be instructed in cases such as these,' said Judge Swinton Thomas.

Here we were, approximately fifteen minutes into my appeal, and already the end was in sight. It came in the following heart-bounding and four-years-too-late terms. I had waited a long and painful time for this moment and it came with mighty force: Judge Swinton Thomas turned up his own volume as he got to the end of the judgement. He concluded:

> Very clearly, however, the written evidence of Dr Whitwell and Mr Wrightson, uncontradicted by the Crown and supported by the expert evidence from the Crown, renders this conviction completely unsafe and unsatisfactory. It is a matter of regret to this Court that the appellant should have been convicted in the first place. Consequently, the appeal must be allowed, the conviction quashed and the appellant discharged.

My feelings were all over the place. I heard what Lord Justice Swinton Thomas said but I could not take it in, probably due to shock at the way the appeal had gone so firmly in my favour even though I had known that it would not be opposed. Judge Swinton Thomas's final words will stay in my memory for ever. I don't know how long it was before I turned to the

Securicor guy and said, 'Is that it? Can I go now?' As I was saying this, the whole of the public gallery began to applaud. Some even cheered and then I got a standing ovation! I caught sight of the two screws from Wakefield – even they were beaming from ear to ear. I made my way to the door that led back down to the cells.

One step outside and 'YES!' I roared. I heard it echo through the building. I lost control of myself now and yelled another mighty 'YES!' What a feeling I had inside me. I'd done it, I'd proved my total innocence, and had brought out many of the unanswered questions about the lack of concern shown to Mandy and the serious symptoms she had shown which had warranted intervention.

When we got downstairs, I was taken to a room where all my belongings were. I tried to take off my jacket but it was hopeless – one of the screws from Wakefield had to help me get it and my tie and shirt off! I went into my box of belongings to find a T-shirt Susan May had sent me, publicising her situation and campaign group. (Susan May was alleged to have murdered her aunt, and is still in prison awaiting her appeal.) I put it on, then my jacket over it while the two screws put my court attire with the rest of my stuff. I had just asked where my legal team were when, all of a sudden, Campbell and Jim Gregory came walking in. 'Where's Michael?' I asked and was told he had had to dash off. I shook hands with Campbell and thanked him for all his efforts throughout my ordeal, then I shook hands with Jim and thanked him too. He had done a lot of behind-the-scenes work on my behalf.

Campbell gave me a statement to read aloud to the media once I reached the outside steps of the court building. I was told to leave my possessions as my family were going to take care of them. I didn't need telling twice, especially as my huge typewriter was in the box.

A copper came in through a door. He told me to stay on the steps otherwise the media would tear me to shreds. It turned out to have been sound advice. Then the side door opened and I saw my family: Mam, Dad, sisters, brother and niece. Only one person was missing: Les. I wished she had been at the hearing.

I gave Mam and Dad a long-awaited hug, then my sisters, my niece and my brother. Judy Ward and Sylvie Carswell were next. I was shaking hands with so many people – I didn't have a clue who they all were – and we hadn't even left the building. I found Mam and Dad again and put an arm round them both. Then we walked slowly towards the steps at the front of the court. Campbell told me to say nothing to all the media people who were waiting outside, just to read the prepared statement once I was on the steps.

We went through some pillars and I caught a glimpse of the cameras that had congregated at the base of the court steps. Jesus, I thought, where have all these come from? I'd never seen so many TV cameras, press and radio all together in one place. Judy came over and said that a taxi was waiting and that my family and I were going to a prearranged celebratory do, the same one that Sylvie had told me about in Brixton.

By now, I was standing on those famous Court of Appeal steps, where other victims of miscarriages of justice had stood. Judy herself had been in this position, so had Paddy Hill as a member of the so-called 'Birmingham Six'. It was good to have them both with me – they would be on hand for me if I hit any difficulties in dealing with the media.

I stopped and took the statement from my pocket. As I unfolded it, I looked up to see a vast array of cameras flashing, the lights of TV cameras glaring and radio microphones almost smothering me. It felt really strange to have this many media people all wanting to hear what *I* had to say. It was also strange that I wasn't at all nervous. It had all happened too fast for that.

I began to read my statement, saying how relieved I was at being free once again, how I had lost a dear child whom I loved, and I thanked the medical team which had been behind my quest for the truth.

Campbell had a protective arm round me to stop anyone trying to ask further questions but even so they were coming from all angles. I remained tight-lipped, as Campbell had instructed me. Now it was time to try to get to the taxi. Judy told me to head straight through the mass of people and before I knew it, I was at the taxi's door and managed to get in, along with my sister, niece, mother, Judy and Sylvie. Cameras were still making a beeline for me but I was safe now. I gave them a clenched fist, which said it all about how I felt at being a free man, and off we drove.

Jesus, what a feeling that was. I was back in society and could have my family around me. In fact, I could do exactly what I wanted now.

CHAPTER

· · · · · · · · · · · · · · · · · ·

11

WHEN WE GOT to the place where we were having the reception for family, friends and a selected few of the media, all I wanted was a cup of tea. I just flopped down. I felt absolutely clapped out.

I talked to all my family and friends in between being filmed and filmed again. I gave interviews from where I were sat and also in an adjoining room. Photos were taken by the dozen, including a lot of me with my family. A news team from New Zealand was there who had kept in the background until now. We had some privacy for this interview, much to my relief, and I was able to thank Philip Wrightson for his efforts and patience in dealing with my endless questions.

By now, it was almost time for the main television news and I sat with my family to watch it. I was surprised that my release was the main headline on the national news on all channels. It was really odd watching myself on the Appeal Court steps reading a statement to the media.

Many more photos later, which included some of my family for the local newspaper in Tameside, someone asked what time I would like to head back for the north-west of England and my home. About an hour, I reckoned, would do just nicely. Meanwhile, I had a long talk with Paddy Hill, who told me what I might be facing now that I had been released. Talking to him was an extremely emotional experience and it felt good that he had taken time out to have a word with me. I also had a long talk with Judy Ward, who had been remarkable throughout my campaign. We agreed to keep in touch and that I would let her know how I was getting on.

We were travelling home on a coach, which had been supplied by Mr and Mrs Armitage whose son was also in Wakefield and contesting his conviction. We went out into the sunshine to walk the short distance to the coach. Sylvie suddenly bounded up to me with a lovely bunch of flowers and put them in my arms. Then, round a corner, I saw the coach. It had my name all over it along with those of other innocent people. A photo of me had been blown up and stuck all over it. Superb, I thought. I said goodbyes to everyone who had come to share this special day with me and we all climbed on. The coach was great and very comfortable, with a drinks machine and sandwiches.

We had a stop at a service area, where some of us had a bite to eat and I made a phone call to Campbell's office. They had all been watching my release on TV and took it in turns to come to the phone and offer their congratulations. Then it was time to get back on the road.

I hardly recognised Manchester when we got there – so many places had been rebuilt or modernised. Cars had changed too – the new Ford Escort was a completely different vehicle from the one I remembered!

I was going to stay with my sister, Janice, for a while until I sorted myself out, but just before we got to Denton where she lived we had to pull up at a layby where a TV team was waiting. They whisked me off to give a live interview, much to the annoyance of my family. Yes, I could have refused to do the interview but I didn't know whether I was coming or going so I just did as they asked.

'We won't keep you a minute,' the TV people said. Well, they were right about that; they kept me about an hour – this at a time when all my family wanted was to see me walk back into a family home. The interview went out live on BBC television. I was asked how I had managed to amass so much specialist knowledge, and how I had coped with understanding all the medical and legal implications of my case; about Mandy's mother, Les, and her support for me; and what I was going to be doing now I was out. At the end they thanked me and ran me back to Janice's home, where a crowd of people was waiting.

Kevin, my brother-in-law, was first to greet me with a massive hug, captured by the press in a lovely photo. Questions were fired at me left, right and centre, but I asked for some privacy with my family. I said I would give interviews later, because I wanted the whole world to know about the gross injustice that had been visited upon two families. The press were happy with that, and left us to it.

We had just had time to make some tea and sit down before the phone started to go berserk. It was the media asking for interviews as soon as I could do them. I agreed to each and every one. I had to keep a sort of diary to know who was interviewing me next, such was the scale of media attention.

Finally we had a breathing space and someone brought me a meal, the likes of which I could only dream about while I was in prison. It was simple enough – chips, burger, peas and bread and butter – but it looked like heaven to me after what I had had to contend with in prison. I made a sandwich with a few chips on, a bit of burger and some peas, but before I got to the end of it, I was feeling as full as a pig. I told Janice I couldn't eat any more and she couldn't understand it. But she didn't know what prison meals were like, how small they are. After a time, your body gets used to having less than normal, so it was no wonder that I was full up so quickly.

Later in the evening, and after even more media phone calls, we all had biscuits and tea. I was to sleep downstairs on the couch, which meant that I could, if I wanted, watch satellite television. Really, I had no choice but to do that: there was no way I could sleep in my new surroundings and my stomach was going haywire – I had terrible pain in my guts. In spite of that, though, just being able to get myself a drink of water without someone asking what I was doing felt out of this world. It was almost impossible to accept that no big steel door was going to close behind me and that no screw was going to check that it was locked. But my guts were really hurting me and I curled up into a ball and tried to concentrate on the TV, although even the sight of tits and bums on the satellite channel couldn't take my mind off the pain. Somehow I got through the night without dying.

Next morning, Kevin was first up at around six. He said he hadn't expected me to be awake so I told him about the stomach pains which I thought were probably down to making the adjustment back to normality. We had a brew and a talk and I told him that, no matter what, Keith and I were going to pay a visit to Campbell Malone's office so that I could thank all his staff for their efforts throughout my wrongful imprisonment.

Nothing could have prepared me, however, for the coverage about my appeal in almost every newspaper that day.

Keith and I went to Campbell's office by bus. It was a tidy journey to his office, entailing two changes, but we made sure we got there early. Before we went in, we found a café where we could have a brew, but then decided to have a full breakfast – a big mistake on my part after the agony of the night before. Needless to say, we ate the lot and I felt like a Sumo wrestler by the time I'd finished. We paid up and took a slow walk the short distance to Campbell's office. Lights were on inside so the staff must have arrived. We walked into the offices of one of the most professional solicitors that anyone could have the privilege of being represented by.

Heads turned. 'Oh, my God!' someone said – and the next minute the whole staff was there to welcome me home. It was beautiful for me as it was the first time that I had met any of them, Linda apart. I gave everyone a heartfelt hug. Over the years, I had formed a close relationship with them all but it was only now that we could each put a face to the voice at the end of a telephone.

All of a sudden TV and press cameras were swarming all over us. How they knew I was going to be there was beyond me as I hadn't told anyone I was going to be at Campbell's office. The girls asked whether I wanted to give interviews or not. No way, I said, and Campbell, who had been told of the invasion, ordered that unless I wished to be interviewed the media people were trespassing and he would take steps to have them removed. Then we got some peace and quiet.

It was a bit like having discovered I had another family and then being introduced to them. Someone asked after Les and I felt sad that she wasn't standing beside me then. Not to be, though, went through my mind.

When Keith and I left, we decided to walk the long distance into Manchester town centre. I don't know why I agreed to this as I hadn't had to walk such a long way in four years and we hadn't got far before I told Keith that my feet were killing me. 'It'll do you good,' he said. And we walked for what seemed like miles and miles.

Along the way I plucked up the courage to ask Keith if he thought Les would be in touch. He felt sure that she would. I got a great lift from that, even though it didn't mean much. He also gave me some wise advice: 'Don't forget – your time has in effect stood still for four years and Les's has not. She has had to make a life for herself. After all, as far as she was concerned you were sentenced to life imprisonment and it's important that you understand what it's been like for her.' I hadn't seen it like that before but it didn't stop me hoping that I'd have contact with Les soon.

*

We headed back to Janice's and along the way people shouted congratulations to me. The best one was when we got to the bus stop in Manchester town centre. A lady came up to me and said, 'Well done, son. This is just what Manchester needed.' I soon found that her words reflected the general feeling of people in the area: other nice comments came my way and I felt glad that I had brought it home to people that miscarriages of justice do happen, even in this day and age.

When we got back to Janice's, there were loads of messages for me from TV, radio, and the press, all of whom wanted me to contact them. I got hold of as many as I could and said the same thing to everyone: any arrangements had to be made through my solicitor, Campbell, who was trying to fit in all the interviews. He had actually advised me to take a break first – it would give me time to clear my thoughts and prepare myself. Looking back, I regret not taking this advice as I'm sure that the amount of time I devoted to the media took its toll on my health.

I had to go back to see Campbell that afternoon. We were going to talk about the way forward for me from here, which would include a review of the case and how to deal with the aftermath. I couldn't wait to see him and it was a joy to set off on the journey to his office.

Once there, Campbell told me that someone was coming in to discuss me appearing on a morning BBC TV programme. I wanted to do this because the BBC had given my case excellent coverage before the appeal. The person from the BBC – Guy was his name – was great and I liked what he said about why I should choose to give my interview to the BBC and no one else – and especially the bit about how I would be looked after! If I agreed to do the show, I would be chauffeur-driven to Birmingham the night before the programme and stay in a hotel. I would be collected the following morning and taken to the studios at Pebble Mill. How could I refuse? I signed a contract, watched closely by Campbell, and Guy seemed pleased.

When he had gone Campbell and I were left to discuss aspects of the case. The question of compensation soon came up and he said he had already submitted a claim to the Home Office. We had had offers from literary agents to represent my affairs – I didn't even have a clue what they did so Campbell had to explain. Finally we came to the most important and exciting media idea: they wanted a live satellite link-up between Philip Wrightson and myself. 'Yes, yes, yes,' I cried to Campbell. 'Let me do it!' This was something I *had* to do. I owed this great man so much for his excellent tuition and patience while I had been studying the brain. The link-up had been scheduled to take place the following morning at the BBC studios in Manchester. Great stuff!

Later, I had to eat another meal and had been wondering all day if this one would cause as much pain as the last and if I would get a night's sleep. I had to face this one whether I liked it or not, otherwise I'd drop dead. I managed a tiny portion. The family thought I didn't like what they were serving up so I had to explain that I couldn't eat because of what had been rammed down my throat for four years in prison. The evening was an action replay of the previous one and Janice gave me some painkillers which eased my guts a little. However, I had another sleepless night. My brain was whirling, mainly with thoughts of contact from Les, which didn't help the stomach trouble because it just added to the stress. One minute I would be all right, the next in severe pain as I was confronted by memories of the horrors of prison plus all the problems I was facing now I was out.

Early in the morning, Kevin came down and was surprised to find me still wide awake and trying to watch TV. He thought I'd sleep like a log once I was home again. But only someone who has been through the nightmare of wrongful conviction can understand exactly what it is like at the time and afterwards. I just hoped that I'd get through the satellite link-up without any serious problems.

Keith went with me in the taxi to the BBC studios, along with an agent from the New Zealand TV station who had requested the link-up. The agent was, surprisingly, very young and we had a laugh on the journey which lasted all of ten minutes.

When we arrived, we went up to the large reception desk and gave my name. 'Oh, yes,' said the young girl, 'we're expecting you. By the way,' she said, 'well done.'

'Thank you very much indeed,' I replied.

More BBC people came up to offer congratulations and we were shown around the studios, which was an eye-opener. Then we were taken to the studio where they were going to do the link-up. It was a very small room and there was a bright light, dead centre between a lot of small TV screens, shining in my eyes. We sat down with Keith to one side of me. An engineer came into the studio and began to explain the procedures but I didn't register anything of what he said as I was too excited about linking up with Philip. This would be the first time that I had seen him.

All of a sudden a picture came on the screen, accompanied by an accent that was as clear New Zealand as you could ever hear. My heart started banging: it was nearly the time when I would see Philip. The picture on the screen was of a studio with cameramen, technicians and lots of people doing the different things which make a studio tick over. I got a big shock when a voice suddenly said to me, 'Well done from all the folk out here in New Zealand, Kevin.' I automatically said, 'Thank you very much,' then heard my own voice a few seconds later on the New Zealand side. Next a voice said that there was a problem. Oh, shit! I thought. Let's have no problems today of all days, *please*. Luckily, they sorted it out and a voice said from the screen, 'Good morning, Kevin.' It was the show's presenter speaking, and the hitch had been due to satellite delay. I was told that we would be live on air in just a few minutes. Great stuff, I thought. I could see the New Zealand side clearly now and knew that one of the people there must be Philip. Which one, though?

'Good morning, New Zealand,' the presenter said. 'This morning, we have a man to speak to in England who has been set free from prison with the expert help of Mr Philip Wrightson, a neurosurgeon here in Auckland. They have never spoken to or met each other until today . . .' Eventually I got to speak to Philip and thanked him from the bottom of my heart for everything. I told him I hoped to be able to get out there and see him. He was much younger-looking than his actual age. He praised my efforts in getting to grips with the intricacies of the medical side of my case, and went on to tell the viewers all about how I had got in touch with him and how he had come to realise that the evidence given at my trial had been so grossly misinterpreted that my conviction could not possibly be said to be safe. It had been brilliant to speak to him after all this time, and I told him I hoped we would be talking again soon.

As we left the link-up studio I was collared by BBC radio to do a live interview. Campbell agreed that the interview could go ahead and I was asked, among other things, how I had found my time in Wakefield and how I had been treated there. The answer to that is elsewhere in this book.

Coming out of the radio studio, I was asked if I would do some filming for BBC TV. Once again Campbell agreed that I could go ahead and I was filmed watching my release. It was the first time that I had seen it on my own and it felt satisfying. I was asked how I felt at the moment of release. What had I felt? I wondered. I said that four years of wrong had at last been put right – but what about Mandy? No one has even said sorry for what happened and 'I don't believe they ever will,' I added. Funnily enough, I haven't seen half the interviews that I have given.

*

Finally – a good few hours after arriving at the studios for the link-up with Philip – it was time to go back to Janice's. Everyone congratulated me and shook hands with me. I'd enjoyed the morning very much – and to the BBC in Manchester I would like to say thank you for the way that you covered my case long before the appeal and for being so hospitable while Keith and I were with you.

Once we were outside the building, I said to Keith, 'You know what? I would have loved Les to be a part of all that's happening. After all, she too has a voice which should be heard as it was her own daughter that all this fuss is about. Having to face it all alone doesn't feel right.' He understood how I felt but reminded me again that Les now had another life to lead, and that if anything was to happen between us now it would have to come from Les's side. I still didn't want to believe that Les had a new life. Keith wasn't going to build any false hopes for me and in this he did the right thing.

Off we went to get the bus. All I could think of was Les. Where the hell was she? I kept asking myself. Then I would tell myself that it had nothing to do with me. Les whirred about in my head all the time. I must have done Keith's head in too because of the amount of time I spent going on and on about her. To make matters worse, my niece, Joanne, worked at a place where she regularly saw Les. I asked her if Les had said anything to her about me. It came as a bit of a shock when Joanne told me she had, so without thinking I asked her to ask Les to contact me. Then I took it back as it was unfair to involve Joanne. I felt sure that Les must be on the same wavelength as me. And must be feeling the pain at what had been done to us all – and especially to Mandy. So many questions that had no answers.

When Keith and I reached Janice's we got a brew sorted out and I tried to eat something but didn't get very far with it. I felt a right plant pot because I'm sure they thought I didn't like their food. Eventually they saw the funny side of my struggle with food. I didn't find it that funny, though, as I was the one who would suffer later.

More people had been in touch for interviews. I couldn't believe that so many papers wanted to talk to me. It got to the stage where I was doing two and three each day on top of TV interviews, which kept me under a lot of pressure and stress and affected my health. I hadn't taken Campbell's advice and was now suffering for my own ignorance. I thought I could just do everything quickly and without any problem but I was now beginning to know just how wrong I had been.

I was absolutely knackered but long after everyone else had gone to bed, I was still watching TV and rolling about in sheer agony. I never had this while I was in prison! Again I remembered what Campbell had said – he made sure himself that I wasn't allowed to forget it: 'You are doing too much too soon.' Again, I endured a lousy, painful and sleepless night. I wondered how much longer I would have all this pain. I couldn't bear to think that it might be long-term.

Another day of freedom dawned but although it felt great to be rightfully free, it was horrible to wonder whether there would be any contact from Les and if I would have to suffer the pain in my belly again. The answer to both these questions was soon to be had. Before then, though, some mail arrived for me, from well-wishers and people who had sent birthday cards. Kevin handed it to me and I immediately gave it back to him. He looked at me so poleaxed that I asked him what was the matter. He said that I had given him back the mail. 'Yes I know,' I said. 'It hasn't been censored.' We all got a laugh out of that one.

It was mid-afternoon when I was told of a phone call that came in for me last night. Who from? I asked. I think you'd better sit down, I was told. Oh shit, I thought. Something's happened to Mam or Dad. It hadn't, though. My nerves got the better of me when they told me it had been Les and I started to walk about the house mumbling nothing and everything to myself. Then I realised I hadn't asked what the call had been about. Les had been upset, I was told. She would call back tomorrow. I was going to Birmingham then so I wouldn't be there. 'Fuck Birmingham,' I said. 'Les is more important.'

Later on, I calmed down a bit. Les had been told that I had to go to Birmingham, where I was to be interviewed on *Good Morning* which meant I had to stay in a hotel overnight. She had asked if I could wait until she had phoned before I left. I hung on as long as I could, even after the driver had come to collect me, but eventually had to leave without hearing from her.

I felt lousy that no call had come and set off in a deflated mood. I soon got my head round the reasons why Les might have found it hard to phone – God knows, Keith had told me enough times. I began to understand that I would have to be patient and simply wait for her.

Now, though, I had to concentrate on the interview I was scheduled to do tomorrow morning. I tried chatting to the driver but quickly went quiet. I just couldn't get Les out of my mind. Would she call again? If she did, when would it be? What time? What day? Would we see each other? All these questions caused me so much hassle because there was no answer. The answer would, or would not, come from Les, if and when she decided to call again.

When we got to the hotel I said goodbye to my driver and went to my room. When I unlocked the door I could hear the TV blaring away. Weird, I thought. This room is booked for me only. I walked in to find Guy there. He must have wanted to make sure that I turned up and to go through a few things in preparation for the interview. We talked about the case and Guy made plenty of notes, especially about the areas Campbell had told me that I must steer clear of: Garrett, Freeman and others directly involved with the case, and compensation too. Then we ordered dinner in the room and watched football on the telly. I asked Guy if he was staying the night at the hotel. He looked at me as if I was daft. 'No, no,' he said, 'I'm going home. I live here.' 'Thank God for that,' I said, and we both had a laugh.

Guy and I got on well and it was a joy to be associated with him. He told me that I'd be picked up at around eight the following morning and taken to the BBC's Pebble Mill studios. We agreed to meet there in the morning and I went off to have a bath.

I made sure that I got to bed early in the hope of a good night's sleep. Some hope. Les was on my mind again and I was already wound up about the morning. It was becoming increasingly clear that I had taken on too much too soon after my release. I'd never known pressure like it, what with all the requests for interviews and worrying about Les and me. Once again, I found myself wishing I'd listened to Campbell's wise advice, because I was finding it harder and harder to cope with all the attention, heartache, worries and stress connected to a miscarriage of justice such as mine.

Somehow I got through the night and was picked up, as promised, from the hotel. It was a different driver this time but he was just as friendly as the last had been. When I got to the studios I was shown to a hospitality area where I helped myself to a brew. I helped myself to a few more after that because it was lovely stuff. I couldn't think of eating anything, though.

When Guy turned up he took me for a tour around the studios and showed me a rehearsal going on on the set of the *Good Morning* programme. Nick Owen, the show's presenter, noticed me in the wings and winked at me. As soon as he had finished his rehearsal he came over to talk to me. He was interested in and knew a lot about my case and I was surprised at just how well informed he was. He is such a nice bloke and very professional in dealing with guests.

After our tour, we were called to Make-up. Guy showed me where to go and introduced me to the make-up girls. I felt such a prat when they put make-up on my face. Jeeze, I'm a boy, not a girl, I thought. They even put hairspray on my mop of hair, which I hated. I got out of there as quickly as I could – maybe they were going to put a frock on me next.

I managed to locate the brew area again! This place would suit me fine, I thought. I had no doubt that when I was needed they would find me easily enough. I didn't have to wait long before a young girl came in with a board under her arm, asking for Kevin Callan. I stood up. 'Ah, good,' she said. 'We're ready for you to be wired.' Fuck me! First, they want me to look like a girl and now they want to electrocute me. It was only when she explained what 'wired' meant that I felt safe again!

She went on to explain how the show was to run that day and went through her notes on the case, looking for reactions from me. I immediately noticed the mistakes. So many had been made by the media in their reports on Mandy's life and death and I couldn't understand why. The facts of the case were easy to get hold of but I began to think that someone must deliberately be giving misleading statements to the press and TV people.

This got to me a bit but I had to concentrate on the inter-view about to take place. I knew I would be asked about Les but I thought this would be easy to deal with. I was going to say as little as possible about her.

It was nearly time for the interview when Guy came to check on how I was. I told him I was looking forward to cor-recting a few so-called facts. He walked me to the edge of the set, where they were broadcasting live, said, 'Give them hell,' and left me to go down to the studio floor.

When I got there, Nick Owen told me that first he would introduce me and then the interview would begin. He would be asking questions on several different issues. Then, all of a sudden, from nowhere, I heard a voice counting down from ten to one. As it said one, Nick began a brief resumé of my release, then said, 'Good morning, Kevin,' and we were off. It all went very quickly, but I made sure I got in the important point about the details that had been reported wrongly in the papers. It gave me great satisfaction to put the record straight about the facts of Mandy's death. I got a surprise when I was asked, out of the blue, 'What does Les think about the case?' and I could only say that I thought she was pleased at my release as she and I had known from the start the full and true facts of the case.

Afterwards I said goodbye to Nick and awaited the call to leave the set. Guy was waiting to take me off for a coffee before I left. He said, 'Well done, it went really well.' Then it was back to Manchester.

CHAPTER

12

WHEN I GOT back to Janice's I spoke to a few people who had phoned as they had seen the programme. More requests had been made for interviews. Les, I discovered, still hadn't been in touch. I spent that evening on the phone, which kept ringing. I wished it would stop, but it didn't. Eventually I answered the phone and heard a voice I recognised: Les. My heart went haywire. We had a brief word about events of late. Then I asked to see her and reminded her that when I was on remand, and still with her, we had made a pact to visit Mandy's grave together as soon as the case was over. We had had no idea that we would have to wait four years. At this point I became certain that Les was being told what to say to me: she was making conditions for her to go to the grave with me. I lost my cool altogether when I actually heard her partner telling her what to say. I felt very hurt and couldn't bear to listen to any more so I put the phone down. Tears filled my eyes when I told the family what she had said. I had waited four years for the right to say goodbye to Mandy and there was no way that I could do it alone. Surely Les understood the importance of us being together when I said goodbye to Mandy. The trouble was that I knew nothing about the demands on her of her relationship with her new partner – and I guessed that he wanted to be present if Les was to visit Mandy's grave with me. This turned out to be true.

Meanwhile, I continued to suffer from stomach trouble and sleepless nights. When I mentioned it to Campbell, he told me that this was bound to happen after the nightmare I had been through. I needed counselling to get over the trauma I had been put through, but I had no money. I received about forty pounds upon release from the Appeal Court, which wouldn't even have got me home.

I had another call from Les, which confirmed my suspicions that her partner had to be present at any visit to Mandy's grave. I told her to forget it unless she could come alone.

When she rang again it was to say that we could go to Mandy's grave alone. That was a tremendous relief. This was something I really *had* to do. Before we visited the grave, though, we made arrangements to meet in her area and Keith ran me to the meeting point where I saw Les and her two kids. I couldn't believe it when I saw Natalie. Four years ago she had only been two; now she was six and I almost didn't recognise her. The other child was Les's younger daughter, born to her present relationship. I was beginning to lose control of myself. I wanted to hold her but she backed off. I pulled myself together and we talked about the case, what would happen about legal action over my wrongful conviction. I told her something had to be done because the medical evidence given at trial had been so grossly wrong. Then I couldn't keep it in any longer and told her how I felt about her still. It made no difference, though. I had to watch her leave to carry on doing her own thing. I stood there crying.

I went back to Keith and sat in the car with my head in my hands. I could see nothing settling me except Les. I told Keith again how much I still loved her and that it was only her who could get me through all this nightmare. The whole case had been about three people only: Mandy, Les and me. I felt it only right and proper that Les and I should help one another.

Keith reminded me, yet again, that Les had her own life to lead, had problems just like everyone else, and that four years was a long time in anyone's life. He always made sense at the times when I felt close to cracking up and I was grateful he was there with me. We made our way home, stopping at the shop on the way for papers and some fags for me. It was my first attempt at spending money since I'd got out and when I came to pay, all I could do was hold out my hand with some money. The notes and coins were all different from what they had been four years ago. I felt an idiot at times like that but most people understood what was happening to me. Little things just added to the pressure on me to readjust – every day it was something different and I didn't know what the hell to expect next. Importantly, I had to get through it with no help from the authorities.

Life went on and I continued to give interviews because I felt it was vitally important that people were aware of the *true* facts of the case. One question came up in nearly every one: I was forever asked how and why I became an 'expert' in neurology. The answer is simple: I knew I was genuinely innocent of the crime of which I had been accused and nothing in this world was going to stand in the way of my proving that, and my relentless search for the truth, no matter how heavy the odds stacked against me. I also had to fight for the truth for Mandy and I felt I owed it to her to get to the bottom of what really went wrong. That was all the motivation I needed to apply myself to getting some basic understanding of neurology, with the help of Philip Wrightson and others. Most of the reports I read in the papers called me a 'neurology expert', which I am not, omitting the words I had spoken during interviews. This caused me great concern: why interview me if they weren't going to print the facts I'd given them? I wondered.

Campbell explained that it was not a case of facts being left out but of fitting the main area of the interview into context. Nevertheless, I saw nothing adverse written about me – quite the opposite.

The hardest part of any interview was talking about Les. All the journalists wanted to know what was happening between us. I could only say that we were apart and that Les would be the one to say if she wanted to be interviewed or not. I was often asked where Les could be contacted but I never answered that one. It was hard, too, to talk about Mandy – and some bits of the story were just too painful to go over again. The press were good to me, though, and understood the sensitivity of the case and my own pain. Sometimes they asked if I had been to Mandy's grave yet. 'No,' I had to reply, but I hoped to very soon. Could they be present when I did so? Definitely not, was my reply, and in this my privacy was respected.

Eventually, I had a call from Les to say that only she and I would be present when we went to Mandy's grave. I wondered why it couldn't have been like that in the first place but it wasn't worth worrying about now – I was so relieved that it was actually going to happen as I had wanted it – and we set a time and place to meet.

When I turned up at the appointed time and place I was delighted to see Les in a good mood. We went to a nearby florists' where I bought a bunch of flowers and I wrote my own message on the card. Standing in the bus queue with Les felt really strange. I couldn't help staring at her: the love I had for her inside me kept trying to burst out. I knew I had to control myself, though, because she was, after all, in another relationship. It seemed that no sooner had we got on the bus than it was time to get off. We were approaching the cemetery and my heart was beating faster and faster.

When we got to the gates, I immediately spotted someone who could only have been Les's partner. I said nothing, just stood still at the entrance and took a deep breath. Tears came into my eyes.

Les pointed in the direction of where Mandy's grave was, in a row for children, and we walked into the cemetery. Words can't describe how I felt but I was racked with the trauma of the past four years. Les stopped. 'This is it,' she said. I went up to the headstone, sat on the grass, and put my arms round it, asking myself the same question I'd been asking myself since Mandy's death: why, why, why? No one could imagine what those moments were like. Les asked me if I was all right, and I said I was, but she knew how I felt – she hadn't really needed to ask.

A little later I told her that her boyfriend was down the hill. She looked back and had to agree that yes, it was indeed him. 'I told him to stay away,' she said. He began to walk up the hill towards us. I told Les to go, that I'd stay for a bit on my own. After a minute or two she went off, unwillingly, very annoyed, to meet him, and I felt that she was going to tell him what she thought of him for turning up where he wasn't wanted.

After she left, I stayed sitting on the grave, taking my time to say my long-awaited goodbye to Mandy. A lady came into the graveyard. I asked her if she had a cloth and she sent a small boy over with one. I cleaned up the headstone and tidied the flowers, which were arranged in little holders. When I had finished, I wrapped my arms around the headstone again and said a prayer for Mandy. I stayed there for another two hours, enjoying being on my own with her. It was hard to leave. I had never felt such pain as I felt at Mandy's grave. No amount of logical reasoning could explain to me why I was saying good-bye to Mandy. I just knew that this was all wrong and that her death should never have happened. But there were no answers. Going to say goodbye to Mandy was the hardest thing I had ever faced.

CHAPTER

13

Now that I had been able to say goodbye to Mandy, I could turn myself to other things, and especially to Sue May's case.* She, too, had been wrongly convicted and I was determined to help her if I could. After my appeal I had worn a T-shirt bearing her name which had caught the media's attention and I told them of the wrongs in her case, which led to good publicity for her. I had decided to visit her at HMP Durham. I wasn't looking forward to being inside prison again but I had promised Sue I would go and go I did.

Durham is a big prison and reminded me strongly of Wakefield. I shivered as I went into the gatehouse and handed in my VO. Lots of people were staring and pointing at me. Nothing wrong in that, I told myself, they just recognise you. Even the screws offered their well dones. Two-faced bastards, I thought. Their colleagues had given me so much shit while

---

* Susan May was alleged to have murdered her aunt. I first read of her case in the 'Conviction' newsletter and I was determined to help her. I was shocked to see that the pathologist in my case had also played a part in hers.

I was fighting my case that I could not bring myself to speak to them properly.

A big rascal of a woman screwess came to meet me and escort me to the women's wing – or so I thought. She asked who I was visiting. 'Sue May,' I replied.

'Well, I'm not taking you,' she said. What a pathetic excuse for a human, I thought.

A male screw appeared and asked who I was visiting. These bastards wouldn't stand a chance on *Mastermind*, I thought, but I said, 'Sue May.'

'Next time you come here make sure you're early,' he said.

'I'm not a prisoner any more so bear that in mind when you speak to me,' I told him. He shut his gob, and on the way to the women's wing, he turned into a caring fella all of a sudden. Here we go, another two-faced bastard, I thought. But I reminded myself I was there to see an innocent prisoner and made sure I kept my thoughts on her.

I was taken through the usual banging, clanging doors. I felt sick as each door slammed shut behind me, and I began to shake as I remembered how it felt to have a door slammed shut and locked until someone else was ready to open it again. I was sweating badly. I was burning up and feeling ill.

At last I was taken into a smart room with tables around it. There were biscuits and brewing stuff on each table. Other people had already arrived for visits and they all turned as I walked in. Jeeze, this is weird, I thought. I sat down at a table and Sue came in. We greeted each other and got straight into the case.

I left that room in some state. How is it that the prison service makes no effort to help prisoners who believe they have been wrongfully convicted? I got out of that place as fast as I could, eager to get back into the freedom that I felt should be Sue's as well as mine.

Shortly afterwards, I met up with Sue's campaign group, the Friends of Susan May, who make sure she is looked after and not forgotten, and gave some interviews on her behalf. Sue's two children, Toby and Katy, have both been brilliant in getting publicity for their mother's case.

Meanwhile, I still had to piece together my own life. Adapting to freedom was far more difficult than I had dreamt it could be. I was still having problems with sleeping and eating but at least I was still breathing, I kept telling myself. The main thing, though, was Les.

Out of the blue, one day, I had a call from her. 'Les, I have to tell you this,' I said, 'I love you more now than I ever did before.' To my astonishment, she said the same to me. 'Well, what the hell are we doing apart, then?' I asked. It wasn't long before we knew that we were going to get back together again. All that I had ever wanted throughout those horrible four years in prison was for Les and me to be together.

Les's dad came to see me to discuss the case, when I told him that any charges arising from it would be initiated by me and that, if she wanted to, Les could join me in any future proceedings against the medical people who had been involved with the case. If we did get back together, I would tell her then of everything she did not yet know, which Campbell Malone and I did, of evidence available to my defence. I made it clear to Les's dad that my feelings for her had never changed and never will, and he and I agreed to keep in touch.

Les and I talked to each other whenever we could. I knew how unhappy she was in her current relationship, but she felt she had to wait for the right time to leave. She would call me when that moment came.

At about eight o'clock one night, I got the call, and about half an hour later she and two children, plus two plastic carrier bags, were with me. I felt like I was dreaming, and I can't describe the joy I felt to have her back. I wrapped my arms around her and didn't want to let her go. When I could tear myself away I told her I had arranged for us to go to my parents' home in Wales for a few days. There weren't any trains that night but my brother-in-law Kevin drove us there. I felt like I was floating.

Mam and Dad were over the moon to see us together again with the children, but we knew we couldn't stay with them for long. During the years of my wrongful imprisonment, they had endured traumas themselves. The strain had been too much for my father's health and he had deteriorated from being healthy and happy to a frail-looking old man who seemed ready to say goodbye to this world, and my mother had recently had a hip replacement.

When Les and I approached the local council, we explained our circumstances and added that my parents were already resident in Wales. I described my parents' state of health and the housing officer agreed that we would be treated as a priority case and that, for the time being, a caravan would be available to us by the end of the week. That was fine by us, and we were told to go back on Thursday to finalise arrangements for the move. Luck seemed to be on our side.

Then, I had to go to the unemployment office to make a claim for benefit for the four of us. What an ordeal this turned out to be. And it was only after we'd filled in all the forms that they told us we had to go to Social Security. We waited half an hour to explain our circumstances, were then given a ticket and told to sit down and wait again until our ticket number came up on an electric sign, which indicated which room we had to go to. It reminded me of prison.

When it was our turn, after what seemed like hours, we were joined in our room by a sorrowful-looking specimen. We could only speak to him through a plastic partition, so I had to shout to be heard. I explained that we had no money and I had only the clothes I stood up in, that we were staying at my parents' but had to be out by the end of the week as they were too ill to keep us with them. I told the man that the State had left us in this position of having no money, no clothes and nowhere to live. 'Leave it with us,' he said. We filled in more forms.

That afternoon, we were lucky enough to receive a payment. A bit of sense, it seemed, did exist somewhere within the confines of the Social Security building, if nowhere else.

At least we had somewhere to live, though. We went back to the housing office that Thursday, as we'd agreed, to pick up the caravan keys – only to be told that, after all, we couldn't have the caravan as the rates for renting one had tripled. Instead, we were given an address of 'suitable accommodation' in the centre of Colwyn Bay – a lovely place at any time of year. We found the house and knocked on the door. The landlady was expecting us, invited us in and sat us down to explain the rules. Then, we were shown the 'suitable accommodation' so generously provided for us. We were flabbergasted at what we saw.

It was at the top of five flights of stairs and consisted of one room with four single beds and a window, which any child could easily open and fall out of. Les was almost in tears so we went back to the housing office. After a two-hour wait, we saw the young girl who had sent us to the 'suitable accommodation'. She was sorry but said that the council couldn't afford to pay the fees asked by the caravan sites. We had an idea. What if we could find a caravan at a price the council would agree to pay? 'Yes,' she said, they would pay it, up to £100 per week.

We went back to Mam and Dad's and told them the news, then set off on our search. We lugged the children all over the place without any luck and in the end, knackered, we decided to call it a day and go back to Mam and Dad's.

When we got there, Mam had worked a miracle. After we'd left that morning, she had phoned the caravan sites and had found one for us at the right price and available for us straight away. She even told the site manageress of our circumstances, so we wouldn't have to go through it all again. We all got into the car and drove the eight miles or so to the camp where we collected the keys and went to see the caravan. Yes! Yes! Yes!

We'll have it! We needed our own space and that would do us just fine. It wasn't the most spacious caravan in the world, but it had a double room and a single with bunk beds, which the kids loved. I was just amazed that what the council had said was impossible – a caravan at £100 per week – my mam had sorted out with next to no trouble at all.

The following Monday we had to change our claim with the DSS. This meant a trip into Rhyl. Again, we had to explain all our circumstances. This time it appeared that we were being understood but again we had to complete a vast number of forms before a claim could be attended to. Handing in the forms, we asked about certain grants, such as a grant for clothing for us all. I had been cleared from the Court of Appeal without any clothes at all apart from those in which I stood. Yet again, we had to fill in mounds of forms.

It was no coincidence that I was still suffering quite severe pain in my stomach. I was under massive stress and all this messing around with forms didn't help.

I was in regular contact with Campbell, informing him of all events we had encountered to date. He was as alarmed as we were at the pettiness of the authorities' attitudes while dealing with us. He asked if I could get to Manchester to see him regarding the case. 'Yes,' I replied, 'so long as I can borrow Mam and Dad's car.' We made an appointment for the following week. Meanwhile, he said, he would get on to the Home Office to address the question of compensation. We certainly needed some finance, urgently. He said he would do all that he possibly could.

I did manage to get to see him the following week and Les also managed to accompany me. I must have looked terrible to Campbell as I was still in some distress. He actually saw the pain that I was in – maybe a good thing really as he was able to assess the damage being done to me and Les. We spoke of a few of the ways in which we could move forward from this point. Some of it went straight over my head. Studying medical textbooks was simple compared to the issues presently being raised by Campbell at that time!

He told me that I would need to see a psychiatrist to formally assess me for long-term and short-term psychological damage. The Home Office would also need to see the report when assessing the level of my compensation. Again, he warned of the dangers regarding taking too much on board. He reckoned that it was much too soon after my release to be going about trying to continue with all the interviews, etc.

'Yes, maybe,' I said, 'but people have a right to know the scale of what really did take place.'

Some of the things that come naturally to most people were causing me quite severe problems. For example, when I went into a shop to buy the most simple things, I could not recognise the value of bank notes. Many times I would give the wrong note. It was the honesty of the shopkeepers that saved me from ripping myself off. Coins too confused me. Since my wrongful conviction, there had been changes to the size of coins: a five-pence piece was now the size of a penny. Such was the change in the year of 1995. Cars made a big impression upon me too. From being a well-versed, knowledgeable car boffin, I soon realised that I was not recognising the most famous cars. When a Ford Escort was pointed out to me I could not believe that they had changed shape so much in such a short period of time. They now looked like something out of the next generation. Buildings, too, were of a new-world design. Road layouts were more than modern. It was like visiting another planet. Was this the real world? I asked myself. Could there have been so much advancement in technology during my time in prison? Or had my world just stood still for four years? No matter what, I had to adjust to the world I was now living in.

While living in the caravan, we still could not hide from the newspapers who had found out where we were. This inevitably led to more requests for interviews. We had more than enough on our plates. We were being dragged through court at every opportunity by Les's ex. He was making allegations that I was a murderer, in spite of the mass of evidence which conclusively proved otherwise, and was alleging that Les was unfit as a mother and that he could care for the children much better than us. We were very worried about my father who was deteriorating rapidly. We were also facing threats from some Manchester people coming down to 'smash the caravan up'. Those people will, I hope, hang their heads in shame. So, with hassle from the press, along with all our other difficulties, things were not exactly easy for us.

I notified Campbell of the hassle we were getting and of the stress it placed upon Les and me. He reckoned that it was best if we charged for any interviews that we gave. At least that would bring some money in. So when we were approached by either TV or press, I requested a small fee after explaining that every interview had, to date, been done for free. We too had to survive just as the reporters did and it was only right and just, in our opinion, that we should not be left without money. Some did pay small fees, others did not want to know. We were very grateful to *Best* magazine and *Chat* magazine for requesting paying interviews. This pulled us right out of the shit. We earned other small fees but nothing that would secure our future – far from it.

As a result of the *Best* interview, we were approached by a TV company. Again, this paid a fee, but nothing to compensate for the work involved. I went ahead with the interview as Les did not want to face up to the cameras. I encouraged her to come, if only to see how it all operated. She declined the offer, instead staying at the caravan. Due to the threats made against us, I tried my all to get her to accompany me on interviews, but she opted to stay put.

This particular interview had me travelling to London. I was collected at 11.30 p.m. and arrived at the overnight hotel at 4.30 a.m.! I was then picked up again at 7.30 a.m. in order to arrive at the TV studios for 8.00 a.m.! After the interview had finished – all of about six minutes – I was taken to Euston to get a train home. I arrived back at the caravan at around 1.00 p.m. This was the time-scale for all interviews in London. Not for the faint-hearted, I thought. Plus, the pain I was in made me look quite an eyesore! Although we were only staying in a caravan, it was bliss to return to it after such a strenuous time.

We were also tracked down by a reporter who represented one of the national Sunday papers. They wanted to do an exclusive story on us and wanted everything. They were only prepared to pay a miserly sum. I was shocked. I told them that should they wish to make a sensible offer then they were welcome to return. Until such time, they were not to make such pathetic offers which, to us as a family, were a disgraceful insult. The reason for us making our start in Wales was to avoid the shit that goes with a case such as this. To be tracked down and have our lives gone over in great detail was bad enough, but to be insulted by stingy offers was like being looked down on too.

Things between me and Les continued in a loving vein. The children were enjoying every minute of their lives here in Wales. Down to the beach we'd go, as well as into Rhyl to allow them (and us!) to go on the rides. There is the Coca-Cola ride in Rhyl, which has a loop on it – you go forwards and backwards and through the loop. Les said that she wanted to go on it.

'Well, you can, but don't dream of asking me,' I said. 'You got me on that stupid boat some years ago and you're not getting me on that bastard loopy loop.'

Needless to say, I fell for Les's old trick again. I reluctantly went on the thing. Down the hill it went to pick up speed. All of a sudden, like a bullet, we were flying through the air and being flung through this loop. At the top of the next hill it slowed down. 'Les,' I said, 'I wanna get off NOW!' She looked at me and laughed her head off. With a big jerk, we were launched backwards to go through the whole process all over again.

Afterwards, it took me about ten minutes to get back on this planet. 'Les, why do I listen to you?' I said. We both had a laugh and kissed. I must be totally bonkers ever to listen to Les when she says that rides are totally harmless. Never again, I say. Well, till next time anyhow!

We were still waiting for the council to find us permanent housing. We went down there many times but found nothing but ignorance. It got to the stage where we had to sit for almost a full day before we got to see somebody. When we did see someone, we were told that, because we had refused the offer of one room for a family of four, then we were to be put at the bottom of the council list. We were eventually told that the council had 'discharged all responsibility for the case'. In other words, they no longer even had time for us. They were certainly not going to re-house us.

Here we were, stuck in a caravan for the foreseeable future. We were more than grateful for it in the beginning, but the lack of space was wearing us down quite fast. We had to be out of the camp by the end of October, no matter what. Meanwhile, we had to try and find somewhere else. With no assistance from the local council, we had our work cut out, to say the least. Still, on we would plod, giving it our best efforts to secure some sort of accommodation.

CHAPTER

·················

14

IN JULY 1995, just a few months after my release, we were paid a visit at night by two cops. They were, they said, investigating the horrendous murder of Sophie Hook which had taken place in Llandudno, some distance away from us. Sophie Hook had been snatched from a tent in her aunt and uncle's garden, sexually assaulted and strangled. They were asking me where I was on such a date and such a time. I was utterly disgusted.

After asking me questions about myself and Les, the police asked if they could take DNA samples from me. This was 'to eliminate me from their inquiries'. I was appalled by the harrowing murder of this young girl but I was equally appalled by their approach to me.

'Is it not enough that you people have subjected me to four years of wrongful conviction? Is it not enough that you have destroyed two families and almost caused suicides within those families?' I asked.

Les came back home shortly afterwards and I told her what had happened. She was gobsmacked – that is putting it very mildly indeed. I called Campbell at home to inform him. He believed I was having him over.

'Campbell, I am not joking,' I said, 'I am very serious. They even want to come back tomorrow and take DNA samples from me. They want to take statements from both Les and me and are awaiting a call from me in the morning after I have conferred with you.' He was silent in his own disbelief at what had taken place. He advised me to go ahead on the basis of having absolutely nothing to hide and said that, because of my horror of the murder and sympathy for the parents, I should agree to be of help in any way possible. But, he said, make it loud and clear that we shall be making a very stern complaint about the situation.

Nothing could have prepared me for the massive shock of the cops' visit. They had put me away four years previously for nothing. Surely, they were not going to try and do it all over again? Here we were, trying to make a fresh start against all the odds and every bit of progress we had made was shattered by their visit. The effects were horrifying. Having gone through a once-in-a-lifetime ordeal already, we now had to try and reach further out to grab at our last hope of normality.

How the hell can anyone find any normality after what we had been through? Even now, as I write about this event, it is close on impossible to describe how I felt. Each and every time I heard a siren I was up and ready for running off. Why, though, I just don't know. I certainly had done no wrong, quite the opposite. Les and I were about to be ripped apart once again, or so it felt to me. We were on our arses when this event took place, struggling to find more suitable accommodation and we were just about keeping our heads above water. We were frightened to death of even walking outside of the caravan, such was the state we were in.

It got so bad that Les was feeling the pressure in a heavy way. I can more than understand why she kept walking away and taking the children. She was so cut up that I found it even more painful to watch her being forced through it again. Why? I kept asking myself. Sadly, no answer was available.

A few days later I went to see Campbell regarding this horrible event and he said that we would add this latest event to the compensation claim. I made it quite clear to Campbell that I had every intention of gaining as much publicity as possible. He told me not to just yet as it might have adverse effects on us. 'Jesus, Campbell, what about the way we already feel?' I said. It felt as if we were totally at the mercy of anyone and everyone who wanted to have a shot at us.

A week later, I could stand it no more. I had to let the public know what was going on. I gave an interview to the main newspaper in North Wales – they had requested one in any event as soon as they found out we were in the area. The lady who came to see me took a great interest in the case as a whole. She was also disgusted at the latest intrusion we had to contend with. She tried to get a quote from the Welsh cops but they refused to comment.

Eventually, in October, Campbell and I met up with the DCI in charge of the Sophie Hook case at Colwyn Bay cop shop. (Someone else had been charged with Sophie's murder thirty-six hours before my visit from the police.) What we were looking for out of our complaint was some form of guarantee that we would not be treated in this way by the police again. I told the DCI that what had happened to us was unjustifiable and no possible explanation could account for the horrendous manner in which the two cops came close to wrecking everything Les, the children and I had built up through extremely difficult times. The DCI explained that the two cops had merely been carrying out their normal inquiries but that, in the circumstances, the police had been at fault and a lesson learned. This made my blood boil. What about the other innocent people who may have been treated in this way? I was told to calm down by Campbell, who rightly pointed out to me that those matters of other people did not have a bearing on my complaint. He requested that we be allowed five minutes alone, to which the DCI agreed. He settled me down but with considerable effort. It was decided that the matter would have to be dealt with by the Police Complaints Authority.

As a result of me giving Campbell heavy earache over the compensation claim, he in turn gave it to the Home Office. I should have had some kind of payment on my release and now, several months later, I had heard nothing. Why is it that convicting the innocent is such a rapid process yet releasing and compensating them takes such a long time?

In late August, after some heavy pressure from Campbell, the Home Office sent us one thousand pounds. They said that this was due to our hardship and was a part payment from any total to be paid. As much as Les and I welcomed this payment, we were impatient to learn how much we were to be awarded and we wanted full compensation as soon as possible.

On the same day, I gave an interview to BBC Wales. This was done in the caravan. I explained how we felt at the way we had been treated since coming to live here in Wales. We felt sick at the disgraceful treatment from the authorities and I gave loud voice to get this message across.

I also gave an interview to a smashing lady, Miss E. Grice, who was a journalist on one of the more reputable national daily newspapers. This article, when it appeared, went down exceptionally well. Many letters of horror were still reaching me where people would voice their disgust at us being left in the position we were in at the time. One lady even petitioned the Home Secretary! I also had a call from someone at Radio 4 who wanted to interview me for a programme called *Cause Célèbre*. I had heard this programme before and was happy to be interviewed for it.

My dad had to go into hospital as a result of a neurological problem. I took him, along with my mother, to Walton Hospital in Liverpool where we were to stay for two days while they ran tests on him. When he came home there were no definite answers as to what the problem was. An appointment was to be made with a neurologist at our local hospital.

Dad's problems had been evident only since my wrongful conviction. Anyone who witnessed him on the Court of Appeal steps could not fail to note that here was a sick man. Indeed, the case had affected many lives and caused illnesses in both our families. Les has told me how she too almost went under. Not in the way I almost went under but in her own way, by taking to drinking heavily. Now, however, she has managed to cut down and only drinks occasionally.

Things began to look up for us in September. We frequented a shop not far from the camp. They were open until ten o'clock at night which came in very handy while living in a caravan. We got to know the people who owned the shop, John and Sandra Bird – it turned out that they were from our area: they used to live in Stockport, the next town to Hyde. As a result of media coverage, they cottoned on to who I was. We soon got on to the subject of the case and discussed all the problems we were presently enduring. I told them that we had to be out of the camp by the end of October and that the council had discharged responsibility for us. John and Sandra made us a fantastic offer – they were building a brand new house facing their shop and offered it to us for an exceptionally low weekly rent. We accepted the offer immediately and it was agreed that we could move in at the end of October. Les and I are indebted to their great kindness and would have been totally on our arses with two kids without the help of John and Sandra.

We had, by now, got both Natalie and Jade, her younger sister, into our local school. Jade would go for two days a week with Natalie going every day. It was great to take them both to school in the mornings as they really did look the part, dressed in their smashing uniforms.

We managed to add to our small collection of household goods when we bought a video. Slowly, we seemed to be getting better and better equipped for when we moved to our new home. However, one day we returned home to find ourselves burgled. The video and stack system had gone. Lots of stuff was scattered all over the show. I went searching for the dirty scumbags who'd done this detestable deed. I found no one about so I called the police, reluctantly. A cop came out merely to tell us that he knew who was doing the robberies and would keep us informed of any developments. I didn't expect to hear from him again which is exactly the way things turned out.

The burglary really unsettled us. We could not get a proper night's sleep again in that caravan. We felt unclean because these scumbags had been in and gone through all our stuff.

At this time, I was also trying to complete my book – an impossible task as there were so many things going on in our lives. The contract for the book was due at any time, as my agent informed me. I needed to get the contract signed and sent back in order to receive part of the advance. This was a whole new world to me – I knew nothing about agents, publishers, editors and the like. Writing this book has been a learning experience. I never thought that there was so much involved, nor did I expect there to be so much interest in my story still. My literary agent also had a lot of interest in the book from TV and film companies.

On 24 October we moved into our new house. We got up that morning with a great surge of expectation. I had deliberately not looked around our new home; I wanted to take the initial steps into it knowing that this was our place. This new home was superb, furnished and brand new. What more could we have wished for? Yes, this certainly felt like our luck was changing for the better. Our first night was spent wallowing in our surroundings. The children loved it, legging it all over the house. They went off upstairs, amazed that they had a big bedroom all of their own, sheer joy evident in their faces. We too had our very own large bedroom – heaven to see a real double bed after all this time of waiting and dreaming about these small things.

We returned to the camp to thank Barbara, the site manageress, for everything she had done for us. OK, the caravan was not exotic, but Barbara had saved us from walking the streets. We bought her some flowers and said our goodbyes. To Barbara I say a very heartfelt thank you for the support you showed us throughout our stay with you.

Soon after we moved, I went up to London for more interviews. One was with a radio station where Michael Howard, the Home Secretary, would also be attending. I could not wait to meet this person as I had some choice words to fire at him. Like, why are we still awaiting a decision from the Home Office about my compensation? Much to my bitter disappointment, I was kept away from him.

I had also been invited to address a seminar of expert witnesses. This is obviously a subject that I feel very strongly about. Experts should, in my opinion, stay inside their own areas of expertise. I was introduced to the experts, and we went through the pitfalls in my case, highlighting the medical evidence. We swiftly ran over what the alleged cause of death was at the trial. We then swept on to the evidence and outcome of the appeal – a totally different conclusion than that of Garrett and Freeman at the trial. I explained my own opinion of the role of expert witnesses in a few words. I hope that talks like this will help alert experts to the danger of wandering into areas where they have no right of entry.

On Sunday, 29 October 1995, I went to collect my daughter, Angela, from Manchester. She was coming to our home for the day, organised by the Social Services in Tameside. We had a smashing day with the three children having a lot of fun. Angela loved the house with its big TV, hi-fi system and lots of gadgets to mess about with.

On the way back to Manchester that night, I had a good talk with her. A date had been set for the direction hearing regarding her and Scott. I explained that, should she want to come and live with Les and me, then that would be fine. If she wanted to go and live with her mother again, that was fine. The decision, as stressed to me by the Social Services, is ultimately her own. What a responsibility to lay on a thirteen-year-old child! However, this was the bare truth and I explained the positive and negative aspects should she choose to come and live here. She listened with interest and appeared to be taking it all very well. Her whole future could be affected by her decision yet she was taking it all in her stride.

No sooner had we set off to take her home, it seemed, than we were there. Time flies when you busy your mind. I gave her a kiss goodbye and told her that I would see her soon.

To me, the days seemed far longer out here than in prison. I now had loads of time to fill, mainly because I had no one behind me everywhere I went. No one telling me that I can't do this or that, can't have certain things – no one running my life, taking all my self-respect away. Not that they ever managed that in prison; they tried hard enough but they now know why I could not possibly bow down to their sad regime.

We had arranged a special bonfire night for the children. We got loads of fireworks for them and they loved their coloured sparklers and all the bright colours. We video-taped it so we would remember a bonfire night which was as enjoyable for us as it was for the children! It was Les's birthday on 8 November. I got her a nice card and took her out to see The Fortunes, Bobby Vee, Gerry and the Pacemakers and Brian Hyland. All on the same bill too!

In November I also managed to speak to Helen Whitwell. I had kept in touch with Philip Wrightson but had not ever spoken to Helen. I was overjoyed when I had the chance to have a long talk with her on the telephone. I brought her right up to date with all events in my life. She agreed to be consulted if we sold film rights and was genuinely shocked at our present situation with the Home Office. After all the time I had spent in a cell, wondering what she was like, I finally had the chance to speak to her. Brilliant!

Because we had talked about the case, it prompted me to call the Home Office. I went berserk when I was told that they were waiting for some paper to be signed. I let rip at full throttle. Is seven months not long enough to wait for them to sort something out? I gave them until the end of the week to sort it out or otherwise I would be camping outside their building with Les and the children!

The following week I was, at last, given an appointment with the psychiatrist at Newcastle. This was now set for 15 November and was confirmed as definite. (I had been due to go several times before but they had kept postponing my appointment.) It turned out to be an all-day session with Kim Fraser. Les had to leave the room in case her presence stopped me from telling him everything. Even so, I could not release all my inner feelings. I believe that it was far too soon for me to be assessed for psychological damage.

Kim understood how I felt about the whole case and the after-effects surrounding me at that time. Even while I was with Kim I had some severe pain in my belly, which was worse when I recounted the more traumatic parts of my case. So many nightmares, so much pain and suffering was endured as I struggled to get the case sorted. That in itself was traumatic enough; on top of that was the despicable regime at Wakefield prison. Jeeze, thinking about it all still gives me nightmares.

It was about 6.30 p.m. by the time we were ready to leave. We were entitled to claim for expenses for getting there and back. To our amazement we were given twenty-five pounds. I'd like to have seen any member of that clinic make the journey from Wales to Newcastle and back for twenty-five pounds!

The following day I received an interim payment from the

Home Office, at long last. Those people just have no idea what it's like to live as we had to. The excuses we heard from them were pathetic at times. But, again, here was another hurdle overcome. We certainly needed this payment urgently as we had suffered enough from the whole case and we needed money to live on.

Les and I were so happy together that we had decided to make it permanent and we set the date for a December wedding. Angela was to be a bridesmaid as well as Jade and Natalie. Angela loved the attention which surrounded her while getting fitted for her dress. I took her back to her foster home and all as she went on about was the forthcoming wedding. She was very happy and proud that we had asked her to be a bridesmaid.

Although everything was going so well, there was one incident that unsettled us and reminded us again that, although I had been proved innocent, I am never free from suspicion.

I had gone to the local Ford garage to pick up my Sierra, which was having engine trouble. The fella behind the desk said that he would go and get the bill. Fine, I said, I will get a brew from the coffee maker. However, as I was pouring the coffee, a hand landed on my shoulder and there were two cops showing me something that could have been an ID card.

'We want a word with you outside,' said this big groucho. I felt in real danger as the pair of them were big lads, to say the least. I had no alternative but to be marched outside. 'We want a word with you about an incident in London from last October,' they said.

'Look,' I said, 'I don't have a clue what you are on about but whatever it is I can tell you that I had nothing at all to do with it. I have come here simply to pay the bill for work done on my car.' They asked to look at my hands. I showed them to these two brutes and they looked at each other then looked at what I presume was a Photofit of someone else. After looking at my hands and the Photofit they agreed that it was not me they were looking for. No matter what, I could not get out of them what this incident in London was. They refused to tell me.

I was, by now, in a state of shock and panic. I could not believe that I had been collared yet again. I tried to tell them that the Sophie Hook episode was bad enough and that I just want to be left alone. I doubt whether they even registered my words. No sooner had they made their horrible presence felt than they were gone. I went back into Ford reception to pay the bill for the car. I got the keys and asked if they knew that the cops were waiting for me. They said that they had no idea.

On the way home I was glued to the rear-view mirror as I was certain that I was being followed. I wasn't being trailed but at the time I was in such a state that I kept veering into the side of the road. I somehow got home but I don't know how. When I told Les what had happened she couldn't believe it. I called Campbell too. He was livid about it and told me to make a statement about it and forward it on to him as soon as possible. Meanwhile, he would contact the DCI we had seen previously and register our complaint with him, along with our complaint about the Sophie Hook episode.

To this present day, I have an in-built warning whenever cops are close by or when I hear a siren. It frightens the life out of me, such is the effect their treatment has had on me.

No sooner had we set the date of the wedding than it was upon us. The day before the wedding, Les was having kittens as she tried to envisage what it would be like. She stayed up all night preparing the buffet we were to have at our home after the wedding. I too stayed up all night. This way we would be together and I could try and answer the many questions that Les had about getting married. What if I say the wrong thing? What if I fall? What if you do a runner? These were just some of the questions she had to ask.

As it turned out, she coped very well indeed. I think her nerves got the better of her as we left for the register office. This was after spending a hectic morning at home with Les's parents, sister and children as well as my brother, Keith. We left the house early. Les went in the Sierra, which was thoroughly cleaned inside and out, complete with ribbon, while I went with Keith. When we got there the Registrar, after explaining the roles of each of us, asked for the money. I looked at Les who looked at me. We exclaimed that we had no money! Next the Registrar asked who the best man was going to be. What best man? Again, I looked at Les with a blank look on my face. Luckily for us, we had Neville, Keith or Campbell to choose from.

I shouted to them to come into the Registrar's room. First of all, I asked Neville to lend me some money, then I said to the three of them that we had no best man and that we requested one of them to stand in. I haven't got a clue to this day whether we did or did not have a best man at our wedding!

I looked at Les, dressed in her brilliant wedding dress. She looked so stunning, even at a crazy, chaotic moment like this. It was with immense pride and love that I was about to make the vows of marriage to a girl in a million.

Once the guests were all in the room, the marriage ceremony began. I rattled my vows off while looking Les straight in the eye. All the love I have for her came pouring out as my vows were spoken. Next, it was Les's turn to make the vows of marriage. She looked a little nervous but she did well. The Registrar pronounced us man and wife. I leant towards Les and gave her a kiss, the very first one as my wife. Excellent!

We had requested a track to be played – 'With You I'm Born Again' – as we signed the register. The certificate was then put into an envelope by the Registrar and handed to us. 'Good luck with your future,' she said. And that was it – off we went, back home to the feast that was waiting for us.

This was one hell of a long day, especially for Les as she

performed miracles in getting everything prepared for the wedding. She had done the lot on her own: bridesmaids' dresses, food, guests, drinks, her own dress, etc. And all this while looking after the children and the home. Jeeze, she really did make the impossible become real.

All round, Les and I found ourselves surrounded by people who genuinely cared and showed true happiness at our marriage on this day. Les's parents looked to me to be very proud of their daughter. I hope that they are also happy that they have a new son-in-law! All the children looked smashing dressed up to the nines. Les's sister, Alison, attended the wedding along with her children, Sophie and Chelsea.

It was late by the time everyone left. It was bliss to unwind after a very tiring and full day. It was even better because I had the best girl in the world as my wife. What more could I possibly want? Waking up on a Sunday morning next to my new wife was a dream come true for me, far above anything I could ever have wished for.

Into 1996 we went as Mr and Mrs Callan. Our complaint to the Welsh cops was still ongoing. We waited and waited for some reply from the Police Complaints Authority. Eventually it came, stating that we had no grounds for complaint. How they can say all this is beyond me. I am now taking civil action against the Welsh cops for their sick and unjustifiable victimisation. It is impossible for me to even begin to accept the PCA's verdict.

There was still a lot of interest in my case from the media. Les and I did our only radio interview together – on Radio 4's *Cause Célèbre*. It went well and Les handled it well, speaking quite openly. My agent had also sold film rights to our story and Les and I met the people who were to make the film.

Things took a horrendous turn for the worse on 10 February 1996. At 2.30 in the morning, I got a call from my mother who was in some distress. Dad had been rushed into hospital.

I could tell that it was serious from her tone of voice so I dashed over to the hospital as soon as possible. The doctor explained that Dad would be lucky to get through the night.

My mind was in turmoil. No fucking horrible way can this be happening to my dad. He does not deserve this. I finally got to see him and stood beside him, holding his hand. The tears were streaming down my face. Dad, I said silently, come on, fight, give it your all. You can't leave us here Dad, not now, not ever.

Some hours later the family was all together and it was as if Dad knew: by some miracle he came to. He saw me and the rest of us and actually asked how Manchester United had got on! He said hello to us all but something was drastically wrong. Through his oxygen mask and all the tubes and wires he began uttering nonsense. I knew that this was not really my dad. I knew that these were his parting words to us.

On 14 February, at 6.25 a.m., my father passed away. My sisters and my mother were with him. They each placed a red rose on him – an act that fills my eyes with tears whenever I think about it.

Dad, we love you today as if you were still with us. You will never be far away from me. I love you.

I was determined to make my dad's funeral extra special. I led the procession into the church to the sound of bagpipes and I organised a display of red and white flowers – the colours of Manchester United – which simply said DAD. At the graveside, I picked up some earth and slowly let it slip through my fingers on to the coffin. I felt like jumping down there to be with him. He didn't deserve to die. His funeral was a service fit for a king, my king.

We went back to Mum's where we all shared in the great and tragic loss of a father and a husband. Mum put her arms around me and said, 'Kevin, you're all I've got now. You remind me so much of your father.' Those words will ensure that I'm never far away from Mum.

*

It wasn't long after this that my own health took a turn for the worse. In June I was rushed into hospital when a duodenal ulcer burst and went through my stomach wall. After an emergency operation I was told that I was lucky to be alive. What an ordeal. The pain was unreal; I have never felt anything like it in all my life.

I am still trying to get back to good health but it is extremely hard, especially as I still have not been offered any form of counselling. The British Judiciary should hang their heads in shame at the way I have been treated.

Les and I are still very much in love. She now has full custody of her two young children and we are still in our rented house. It hasn't been easy for us, but we're still in there and going strong.

When this book is published and the film shown, I hope people will see the reality of what a case like mine can do to a family. I can only hope that the reader is never subjected to the ordeal that I went through.

EPILOGUE

·················

DURING THE WRITING of this book, I have relived my nightmare. Not all of it was bad – recounting my marriage to Les brought me great happiness – but at times I have had to stop writing for a while because of the pain it caused me. Sometimes I wondered why I was putting myself through it. I think the answer is evident within these pages.

Wakefield certainly opened my eyes in a big way. I would never have believed that humans could be treated as badly as they were in that hell-hole. Nothing can describe how I felt at the way I was treated in that prison. I often wonder how they feel now that I am back where I belong, and I hope no other innocent people are suffering what I went through. Wakefield still gives me many horrendous nightmares and I have nothing but bad memories of that place. No, I shall never forget it.

I shall remember all the people I wrote to while at Wakefield, some of them negative, but most of all I shall remember my own experts for their valuable assistance. I got out of prison because of many things. Number one was that I was innocent. Obtaining the evidence to prove it was, however, very traumatic indeed and I could not have done it without their help.

I played no part in Mandy's death and I shed many tears at the wrong of it all. I also shed many tears as I began to receive the evidence required to set me free. I have to say that other innocent victims are not so fortunate as me. I am lucky enough to have my family around me. We overcame the odds and came through.

To the innocent people: do not ever give up. There is always a way – let me be evidence of that. I hope that the reader can find hope and strength in the pages of this book. I have shown that odds mean nothing. Each of us can reach out and make a lot of meaning out of nothing. I did. So can you.